THE PASSION TRANSLATION

THE PASSIONATE LIFE BIBLE STUDY SERIES

12-LESSON STUDY GUIDE

THE BOOKS OF

TITUS AND PHILEMON

LIVING FOR GOD

tPt

BroadStreet PUBLISHING

BroadStreet Publishing® Group, LLC
Savage, Minnesota, USA
BroadStreetPublishing.com

TPT: The Books of Titus and Philemon: 12-Lesson Bible Study Guide

9781424571741 (softcover)
9781424571758 (ebook)

General editor: Brian Simmons
Managing editor: William D. Watkins
Writers: Andrew P. Kauth and William D. Watkins

Cover and interior by Garborg Design Works | garborgdesign.com

Printed in China

26 27 28 29 30 5 4 3 2 1

Contents

From God's Heart to Yours

"God is love," says the apostle John, and "Everyone who loves is fathered by God and experiences an intimate knowledge of him" (1 John 4:7). The life of a Christ-follower is, at its core, a life of love—God's love of us, our love of him, and our love of others and ourselves because of God's love for us.

And this divine love is reliable, trustworthy, unconditional, other-centered, majestic, forgiving, redemptive, patient, kind, and more precious than anything else we can ever receive or give. It characterizes each person of the Trinity—Father, Son, and Holy Spirit—and so is as limitless as they are. They love one another with this eternal love, and they reach beyond themselves to us, created in their image with this love.

How do we know such incredible truths? Through the primary source of all else we know about the one God—his Word, the Bible. Of course, God reveals who he is through other sources as well, such as the natural world, miracles, our inner life, our relationships (especially with him), those who minister on his behalf, and those who proclaim him to us and others. But the fullest and most comprehensive revelation we have of God and from him is what he has given us in the thirty-nine books of the Hebrew Scriptures (the Old Testament) and the twenty-seven books of the Christian Scriptures (the New Testament). Together, these sixty-six books present a compelling and telling portrait of God and his dealings with us.

It is these Scriptures that *The Passionate Life Bible Study Series* is all about. Through these study guides, we—the editors and writers of this series—seek to provide you with a unique and welcoming opportunity to delve more deeply into God's precious Word, encountering there his loving heart for you and all the others he loves. God wants you to know him more deeply, to love him more devoutly, and to share his heart with others more frequently and freely. To accomplish this, we have based this study guide series on The Passion Translation of the Bible, which strives to "reintroduce the passion and fire of the Bible to the English reader. It doesn't merely convey the literal meaning of words. It expresses God's passion for people and his world by translating the original, life-changing message of God's Word for modern readers." It has been created to "kindle in you a burning desire to know the heart of God, while impacting the church for years to come."[1]

In each study guide, you will find an introduction to the Bible book it covers. There you will gain information about that Bible book's authorship, date of composition, first recipients, setting, purpose, central message, and key themes. Each lesson following the introduction will take a portion of that Bible book and walk you through it so you will learn its content better while experiencing and applying God's heart for your own life and encountering ways you can share his heart with others. Along the way, you will come across a number of features we have created that provide opportunities for more life application and growth in biblical understanding.

Experience God's Heart

This feature focuses questions on personal application. It will help you live out God's Word and to bring the Bible into your world in fresh, exciting, and relevant ways.

Share God's Heart

This feature will help you grow in your ability to share with other people what you learn and apply in a given lesson. It provides guidance on using the lesson to grow closer to others and to enrich your fellowship with others. It also points the way to enabling you to better listen to the stories of others so you can bridge the biblical story with their stories.

The Backstory

This feature provides ancient historical and cultural background that illuminates Bible passages and teachings. It deals with then-pertinent religious groups, communities, leaders, disputes, business trades, travel routes, customs, nations, political factions, ancient measurements and currency…in short, anything historical or cultural that will help you better understand what Scripture says and means.

Word Wealth

This feature provides definitions for and other illuminating information about key terms, names, and concepts, and how different ancient languages have influenced the biblical text. It also provides insight into the different literary forms in the Bible, such as prophecy, poetry, narrative history, parables, and letters, and how knowing the form of a text can help you better interpret and apply it. Finally, this feature highlights the most significant passages in a Bible book. You may be encouraged to memorize these verses or keep them before you in some way so you can actively hide God's Word in your heart.

Digging Deeper

This feature explains the theological significance of a text or the controversial issues that arise and mentions resources you can use to help you arrive at your own conclusions. Another way to dig deeper into the Word is by looking into the life of a biblical character or another person from church history, showing how that man or woman incarnated a biblical truth or passage. For instance, Jonathan Edwards was well known for his missions work among native American Indians and for his intellectual prowess in articulating the Christian faith, Florence Nightingale for the reforms she brought about in healthcare, Irenaeus for his fight against heresy, Billy Graham for his work in evangelism, Moses for the strength God gave him to lead the Hebrews and receive and communicate the law, and Deborah for her work as a judge in Israel. This feature introduces to you figures from the past who model what it looks like to experience God's heart and share his heart with others.

The Extra Mile

While The Passion Translation's notes are extensive, sometimes students of Scripture like to explore more on their own. In this feature, we provide you with opportunities to glean more information from a Bible dictionary, a Bible encyclopedia, a reliable Bible online tool, another ancient text, and the like. Here you will learn how you can go the extra mile on a Bible lesson. And not just in study either. Reflection, prayer, discussion, and applying a passage in new ways provide even more opportunities to go the extra mile. Here you will find questions to answer and applications to make that will require more time and energy from you—if and when you have them to give.

As you can see above, each of these features has a corresponding icon so you can quickly and easily identify them.

You will find other helps and guidance through the lessons of these study guides, including thoughtful questions, application suggestions, and spaces for you to record your own reflections, answers, and action steps. Of course, you can also write in your own journal, notebook, computer document, or other resource, but we have provided you with space for your convenience.

Also, each lesson will direct you toward the introductory material and numerous notes provided in The Passion Translation. There each Bible book contains a number of aids supplied to help you better grasp God's words and his incredible love, power, knowledge, plans, and so much more. We want you to get the most out of your Bible study, especially using it to draw you closer to the One who loves you most.

Finally, at the end of each lesson you'll find a section called "Talking It Out." This contains questions and exercises for application that you can share, answer, and apply with your spouse, a friend, a coworker, a Bible study group, or any other individuals or groups who would like to walk with you through this material. As Christians, we gather together to serve, study, worship, sing, evangelize, and engage in a host of other activities. We grow together, not just on our own. This section will give you ample opportunities to engage others with some of the content of each lesson so you can work it out in community.

We offer all of this to support you in becoming an even more faithful and loving disciple of Jesus Christ. A disciple in the ancient world was a student of her teacher, a follower of his master. Students study, and followers follow. Jesus' disciples are to sit at his feet and listen and learn and then do what he tells them and shows them to do. We have created *The Passionate Life Bible Study Series* to help you do what a disciple of Jesus is called to do.

So go.

Read God's words.

Hear what he has to say in them and through them.

Meditate on them.

Hide them in your heart.

Display their truths in your life.

Share their truths with others.

Let them ignite Jesus' passion and light in all you say and do.

Use them to help you fulfill what Jesus called his disciples to do: "Now wherever you go, make disciples of all nations, baptizing them in the name of the Father, the Son, and the Holy Spirit. And teach them to faithfully follow all that I have commanded you. And never forget that I am with you every day, even to the completion of this age" (Matthew 28:19–20).

And through all of this, let Jesus' love nourish your heart and allow that love to overflow into your relationships with others (John 15:9–13). For it was for love that Jesus came, served, died, rose from the dead, and ascended into heaven. This love he gives us. And this love he wants us to pass along to others.

Why I Love the Letters of Titus and Philemon

God's grace shines through these two books, Titus and Philemon. In the grand collection of Scripture, some books shout, and some whisper. Some unveil the majesty of God's plan on a cosmic scale, and others speak like a spiritual father sitting across the table, offering wisdom forged in the fires of love and discipleship. Titus and Philemon fall into the latter category. These letters may be short in length, but they are deep wells of insight for any lover of God who longs to reflect Christ in the practical rhythms of life.

Titus: Truth That Transforms Character

Alongside Paul's letters to Timothy, the letter to Titus belongs to what is traditionally called the Pastoral Epistles. But make no mistake—the pastoral wisdom of Titus isn't limited to pulpit or platform. It is rich, relevant, and razor sharp for anyone who desires to live a life pleasing to the Lord.

Paul's words to Titus carry the seasoned voice of a spiritual father passing the torch to a trustworthy son. His exhortations are laced with urgency, not just to get doctrine right but to live rightly before God and people. This is what I love most about Titus—it bridges sound teaching with sound living.

Take Titus 2:11–12, for example: "For the grace of God has appeared, bringing salvation to all men, instructing us to deny ungodliness and worldly desires and to live sensibly, righteously and godly in the present age." Paul rooted godliness in grace. His letter provides no dry list of moral checkboxes. Instead, it presents the fruit of grace at work in a soul that has seen Jesus. The gospel that saves is the same gospel that sanctifies. Titus reminds us that holiness is not merely avoiding sin but also embodying the beauty of Jesus in every arena of life—home, church, and public square.

From elders to young women, from slaves to leaders, Titus paints a picture of a community shaped by heaven's values. Every relationship, every attitude, and every action become an opportunity to "adorn the doctrine of God our Savior" (Titus 2:10). That's the kind of discipleship I crave—a lifestyle that makes grace visible.

Philemon: The Gospel in Real Time

Then comes Philemon—Paul's shortest letter, but arguably one of his most personal and powerful. While Titus offers instruction for leadership and godly living, Philemon shows the gospel in action. It's the story of Onesimus, a runaway slave who encounters Jesus and becomes a brother in the Lord. Paul sends him back, not as a fugitive but as family.

What I love about Philemon is its sheer tenderness. Paul didn't command Philemon; he appealed to him on the basis of love. He invited him to do the unthinkable in that cultural context—receive a slave as a beloved brother. This letter isn't just about social dynamics—it's about transformation. It's a picture of redemption that touches real life.

Philemon teaches that no person is beyond the reach of Christ. It challenges us to rethink relationships through the lens of grace. How do we treat people who have wronged us? How do we view those society labels as lesser? In Philemon, we see that the gospel not only reconciles us to God but to one another.

Practical Application for the Lover of God

Here's why these two letters grip my heart as a lover of God. They call me to live what I believe. Doctrine is not just for study—it's for transformation. Titus reminds me that grace trains me to live in a way that glorifies God in the everyday.

These letters also challenge me to lead by example. Whether in the home, church, or workplace, these letters call me to integrity, humility, and courage—to be someone others can follow as I follow Christ.

They compel me to love beyond comfort. Philemon invites me to forgive, restore, and value people as God does, even when it's costly or countercultural.

They reveal the beauty of spiritual family. Both books speak to relationships, not just in terms of roles but of love—spiritual fathers and sons, brothers and sisters in the faith, living in mutual honor.

In a world of conflict and distraction, Titus and Philemon offer grounded, Spirit-breathed direction. They remind me that the gospel is not just something I proclaim—it's something I embody. Whether I'm discipling a friend, resolving a conflict, or simply trying to be faithful in the small things, these letters draw me back to the heart of God.

A Final Word

If you love God and long to see his image formed more deeply in your life, spend time in the books of Titus and Philemon. Don't rush through them. Linger. Listen. Let the Spirit of God highlight what he wants to form in you. And remember: the same grace that appeared and brought salvation is the grace that teaches us how to live.

May we be like Titus, faithful to what we've been entrusted with. And like Philemon, willing to embrace others the way Christ embraced us.

Brian Simmons

General Editor

LESSON 1

Introduction to Titus

(Titus 1:1–4)

Along with Paul's two letters to Timothy, Paul's letter to Titus is part of what is traditionally referred to as the Pastoral Epistles—letters written by a spiritual father (Paul) to his spiritual sons (Timothy and Titus). And like 1 and 2 Timothy, Titus is significant for its pastoral instructions.

As you read through Titus, you'll encounter verse after verse of not only pastoral wisdom but also godly, seasoned advice that will be relevant for you, whether you're involved in Christian ministry as a church planter, pastor, lay minister, or you're simply a follower of Jesus looking to pursue a greater measure of holiness in your life. As you journey through the epistle of Titus, you'll experience a fresh understanding of what it means to have every aspect of your life reflect God's saving grace—from your relationships with your family and church to the relationships you have with everyone else in your daily life.

Authorship, Date, and Recipient

Paul's authorship of Titus is relatively uncontested in modern scholarship, and the date of its composition typically only sees two widely accepted opinions: AD 57 or sometime between 62 and 64. And while the greater level of support falls on a later time frame, Bible commentator John Whittaker contended that "it's possible to see both 1 Timothy and Titus as written on Paul's 3rd missionary journey around A.D. 57, during the 6 months to a year that he traveled through Macedonia and Illyricum after he left Ephesus and before wintering in Corinth (see Acts 20:1–3)."[2] If, on the other hand, Paul wrote to Titus in the early 60s, it's safe to assume that he wrote to Titus from Corinth or Nicopolis. This would have been between Paul's first and second imprisonments in Rome and while he ministered to the churches in Macedonia. As Bible teacher John MacArthur stated:

> Most likely, Titus served with Paul on both the second and third missionary journeys. Titus, like Timothy (2 Tim. 1:2), had become a beloved disciple (1:4) and fellow worker in the gospel (2 Cor. 8:23). Paul's last mention of Titus (2 Tim. 4:10) reports that he had gone for ministry in Dalmatia—modern Yugoslavia.[3]

Regardless of the letter's date, it's clear that Paul was writing to Titus in support of his ministry work in Crete as an evangelist, church planter, pastor, and church leader. Titus himself is mentioned in the New Testament thirteen times, with his earliest mention found in Galatians 2:1, where Paul wrote, "Fourteen years later, I returned to Jerusalem, this time with Barnabas and Titus, my coworkers." Chronologically, this would place Titus as traveling with Paul about fifteen years prior to when Paul wrote his letter to Titus. That's not an insignificant detail because it shows the depth of the relationship between Paul and Titus, pointing out that Titus was not only one of Paul's early ministry partners but also very likely his longest (preceding Timothy and outlasting Barnabas).

An investigation into the various mentions of Titus in the rest of the New Testament will find the majority of the references recorded in 2 Corinthians. Pastor Brian Dennert summed them up nicely:

> He [Titus] visited Paul and comforted him with his presence but also with his words about the Corinthians' care and concern for Paul (2 Corinthians 7:6–7). Titus was also encouraged by the Corinthians in his time with them (7:13) and seems to have a genuine care for the Corinthians (8:16). Part of his work with the Corinthians was encouraging them to participate in the collection that Paul was making to help the church in Jerusalem—an important task that Titus did not seem to resent at all but was eager to do (8:6, 16–17). Paul also notes that he had sent Titus to see them, showing his trust in him, and that Titus acted in integrity in his time with them (2 Corinthians 12:18[4]). Overall, the references to Titus's work in this letter reflect the label that Paul gives him as a "partner and fellow worker" (8:23).[5]

- *What would you conclude about Titus's character and commitment to Paul and his ministry from the preceding description of Titus?*

- *Have you ever had someone like Titus working with you? If so, who was it and how would you describe him or her?*

Purpose and Themes

Paul sought to offer specific guidance to Titus through writing this letter—guidance that would be useful to his ministry in Crete. As Paul told Titus at the start of his letter, "I'm writing to you to further the faith of God's chosen ones and lead them to the full knowledge of the truth that leads to godliness" (1:1).

- *In verse 1, to whom is Paul referring when he charges Titus with the task of furthering the faith of "God's chosen ones"?*

- *As you consider how to apply Paul's counsel to his protégé, Titus, who would be "God's chosen ones" in your life? What is your role in their lives?*

- *Read Titus 1:1–3. What do these verses reveal about God? (Be sure to check out the TPT footnote on verse 2.)*

- *What do these opening verses tell you about "the truth" and its importance?*

- *What was Paul entrusted with and by whom (v. 3)?*

- *How does Paul describe Titus (v. 4)?*

- *What does Paul's blessing over Titus say about God and Jesus (v. 4)?*

- *Now read through the rest of this short letter, noting what you find as the letter's major themes and writing them down here.*

In TPT's introduction to Titus, you'll find three major themes of this letter: (1) "faith and salvation in Jesus Christ," (2) "appointing church leadership," and (3) "right living for the sake of the gospel." In addressing faith and salvation in Jesus Christ (the first theme), Paul offered a summary of the basic beliefs of Christianity throughout Titus' three brief chapters. Paul also talked about church leadership (the second theme), which is important to encouraging godly living (the third theme). Indeed, without solid leadership, believers—and especially new believers—will lack the appropriate resources as they are discipled, especially in the face of a culture very much opposed to Christianity and ripe with false teaching. And that is as true today as it was in the days of Paul and Titus.

- *What do you see as the basic beliefs of Christianity? More specifically, if you had to condense the tenets of Christianity down to a list of a few nonnegotiable beliefs, what would those be?*

- *What are some of the qualities that you admire in the various leaders that you've had in your life (think of parents, relatives, pastors, missionaries, teachers, coaches, etc.)?*

- *What are the characteristics you look for in a leader of a church or parachurch ministry?*

EXPERIENCE GOD'S HEART

As you study Titus, you'll experience the many aspects of God's heart for you: his deep love, his patience as you learn to grasp the depths of his grace, and his desire for you to seek holiness. In Titus 1:1–2, Paul wrote that "godliness…rests on the hope of eternal life."

- *How does your current understanding of God and his heart for you impact the way in which you live your life?*

- *Make it a personal goal, as you study your way through Titus, to deepen your understanding of God and his heart for you. How might a simple desire to more fully understand these matters encourage you to pursue holiness and influence your day-to-day life?*

SHARE GOD'S HEART

Have you ever been assigned a task so important that it consumed all you did, whether that particular charge had to be completed in the short- or long-term? Paul gave Titus quite the task in Titus 1:1—an important work that involved leading the Christian church on an entire island. As you read through Titus, consider the monumental task this ministry partner of Paul had to undertake as he sought to spread the gospel and disciple believers on the island of Crete.

- *In the past, how have you prepared to take on projects that, at the outset, seemed extraordinary, certainly a challenge or stretch of your abilities?*

- *How might Titus 1:4 have served as an encouragement to Titus?*

- *How can you use that same verse as encouragement in your own life, especially as you share God's heart with others?*

Talking It Out

Since Christians grow in community, not only in solitude, here are some questions you may want to discuss with another person or in a group. Each "Talking It Out" section is designed with this purpose in mind.

1. Read TPT's "About Titus" section in its "Introduction" to the letter. What did you learn there that wasn't covered in this lesson?

2. In the "About Titus" section, it says that "the theme of Titus is that right living will always accompany right doctrine." What do you see as the relationship between believing true Christian teaching and living the Christian life? What do beliefs (what we accept as true) have to do with living life?

3. Many consider the epistle of Titus to be a kind of church-planting manual. Even if you have no desire to plant a church or be involved in full-time ministry, how can delving into such a topic be useful in your Christian life?

LESSON 2

Church Leaders

(Titus 1:5–9)

Have you ever tried to straighten something that was bent? Were you able to make it just as straight as it was prior to it being bent?

Here's another situation that you may find familiar: continuing to drive on a flat tire. If you've ever done that, you almost certainly upset your preferred mechanic or any of your mechanically inclined friends. When you get a flat tire, you need to pull over as soon as possible. Why? Well, it's not easy to fix a bent rim.[6] Unless you're an expert with the right tools, you're going to struggle.

Or consider this: have you ever had to move yourself and your belongings from one geographical location to another? At the very least, moving requires that you organize everything that needs to be packed up and then find a place for everything and put it all away after unpacking. Moving is always quite a feat, especially if you have a family.

Any of these situations could cause significant angst, especially if you've rarely experienced them and aren't a professional at any of them.

In any event, this is the idea behind the task that Paul assigned Titus. Paul gave him the goal of straightening out the Christian community on the island of Crete: "The reason I stationed you in Crete was so that you could set things in order and complete what was left unfinished" (1:5). Titus' main task, in fact, was to restore order in the Cretan churches, making certain that the leadership was duly qualified. And that specifically meant that Titus was in charge of appointing church leaders. Definitely quite the project!

- *Think about an important task or a difficult job that you either took on in the past or even somewhat recently. What was it? How did you feel at the outset, and would you say that you were successful in completing the task or finishing the job?*

- *What qualities do you feel you possess that generally allow you to take on difficult things well? If you don't consider yourself that type of person, what aspects of your personality do you think you'd need to refine in order to do better when faced with important challenges?*

- *Considering Titus' job in Crete, what character traits do you believe he would need to possess? (As you consider your answer to this question, don't simply pull answers from verses 5–9.)*

WORD WEALTH

In order to gain a more complete understanding of Paul's qualifications for church leaders, which he briefly outlines in verses 6–9, it's important to define the word *elders* that he used in verse 5 and the word *overseer* that he used in verse 7.

The Greek word translated "elders" in verse 5 is *presbyteroi*, the plural form of *presbyteros*. The *presbyteroi* were elders.[7] And notice that Paul told Titus to raise up and appoint elders "in every city," not in every church. Christian elders in Paul's day were similar to Jewish elders. In the first century, Jewish elders were "predominantly the aristocratic leaders of the Jewish patrician families. They served in local village councils and alongside the Pharisees and Sadducees in the Sanhedrin, the great council of Jews in Jerusalem."[8] In other words, Jewish elders were older respected community leaders. Likewise, *Christian* elders were community leaders too, looking out for all of the Christian house churches in the community in which they served.

At this time in history, there were no buildings erected to be only places of Christian worship. In fact, no such buildings existed until after the Edict of Milan was issued in 313 by the Roman emperor Constantine. This decree provided for religious freedom throughout the Roman Empire, allowing Christians to finally erect structures for the sole purpose of Christian worship.[9] So when Paul wrote Titus in the middle of the first century, Christians met in homes, not in dedicated church buildings, and their homes housed not only family members but also often "slaves and friends, tenants, [and] partners or clients who would have been involved in a common commercial or agricultural enterprise."[10] In a first-century city, several house churches existed, and it was the elders who provided sources of wise oversight over all of the house churches in a certain locale.

Paul, however, did not just mention elders. In Titus 1:7, he also named the "overseer." The Greek word he used is *episkopos*, which is usually translated "overseer" or "bishop." Some Bible scholars think that Paul used this word to refer to the same leaders he talked about in verse 5: namely, elders. But many Bible scholars see *episkopos* as a different church leader than elder. Increasingly, Bible scholars see the *episkopos* as the head of the family in the home where believers met. In other words, the homeowners of each house church were the host leaders of the group of Christians who met in their residence. They provided direct pastoral oversight of the believers who gathered under their roof.[11] New Testament scholar C. G. Kruse summarized the first-century situation this way: "Bishops were the hosts of the house churches and they exercised a supervisory role over the church meeting in their houses. Elders were leaders in the Christian community, but were not necessarily hosts of house churches as well."[12]

- *Let's learn more about the presence and place of house churches in the New Testament period. In the following chart, (1) read the passage listed in the left-hand column; (2) in the next column to the right, provide the name and/or description of the house church owners/hosts; (3) in the next column, jot down who gathered in that house church and what they did there; and (4) in the last column note where the house church was located (hint: the context of the passage or the destination of the letter usually provides the answer of location).*

Early House Churches

Bible Passages	Names and Descriptions of Homeowner(s)/ Hosts	Who Gathered There and What They Did	City/ Region of the House Church
Acts 2:46			
Acts 12:12–17			

Acts 16:40			
Romans 16:3–5			
Romans 16:23			
1 Corinthians 16:19			
Colossians 4:15			
Philemon 1–2			
2 John 10			

- *What did you learn about these house churches and their owner hosts? Did anything surprise you? If so, what?*

Qualifications of Elders and Overseers

Let's consider what Paul had to say about the church leadership positions of elder and overseer.

Elders

Paul had some very specific instructions for Titus as he established "church elders in every city" (Titus 1:5). As Titus set about organizing the Christian church in Crete, Paul wanted to make sure the leaders were up to God's standards—what Paul called "above reproach" (v. 6).

- *Describe a leader you would consider "above reproach," whether that leader was/is a church leader (pastor, elder, Bible study leader, etc.) or a secular leader (maybe a coach, teacher, or boss). What characteristics and qualities stand out to you?*

- *Do you personally hold leaders in churches to higher standards than Christians who are not in leadership? What about leaders who are Christians but not holding an official church leadership position? What standards do you think they should hold to and exhibit?*

- *Go through the following list of qualifications and write down what each of them means to you. Aim for simple, easily understood definitions and jot down examples that connect to your own experience/understanding.*

  Be "devoted solely to his wife" (v. 6).

  Have children who "are believers and not rebellious or out of control" (v. 6).

- *Given what you now know about house churches and who elders were, why do you think Paul highlighted these two requirements along with being above reproach? Why would these requirements matter for Christians meeting in house churches?*

- *For a church that's not a house church, do you think these requirements are still important for at least some church leaders? Why or why not?*

Overseers

Paul then turned to overseers and the qualifications that they should meet.

- *As you did with elders and their qualifications, work through the following list of qualifications for overseers and write down what each of the qualifications means to you. Keep your definitions simple and provide examples that connect to your own experience/understanding.*

  Possess a "blameless character" (v. 7).

  "Not be opinionated or short-tempered" (v. 7).

  "Not be a drunkard or violent or greedy" (v. 7).

  Be "known for his hospitality" (v. 8).

  Be "a lover of goodness" (v. 8).

  Be "fair-minded, pure-hearted, and self-controlled" (v. 8).

"Have a firm grasp of the trustworthy message that he has been taught" (v. 9).

Be able to "encourage others with healthy teachings and provide convincing answers to those who oppose his message" (v. 9).

- *Once again, think about the house church environment and the overseers, or homeowner hosts. Why would the previous qualifications of leadership matter in a house church situation? Why would overseers need such qualifications in their roles?*

- *For leaders who are not leading house churches, do you think that these qualifications still matter? Why or why not?*

EXPERIENCE GOD'S HEART

One aspect of God's heart for his followers relevant to Titus 1:5–9 is that you (his people) would be holy. Consider this verse from Deuteronomy: "'For you are a people holy to the LORD your God. The LORD your God has chosen you to be a people for his treasured possession, out of all the peoples who are on the face of the earth'" (7:6 ESV).

- *How can aspiring to live like one who is qualified to be a church leader help you to live a life marked by holiness?*

- *When you consider all that Paul wrote about in Titus 1:5–9, what qualities of church leadership do you feel are the most important in the pursuit of obtaining holiness and God's heart for you?*

SHARE GOD'S HEART

- *Verse 6 talks about church leaders being above reproach. How does a life lived above any and all reproach serve a Christian as he or she lives in a secular society (whether involved in leadership or not)?*

- *Reread verses 7–8. Hospitality shows a deep care for others and reflects God's welcoming heart toward all people. How are you making space in your life to love others in this way?*

- *Verse 9 mentions having "a firm grasp of the trustworthy message." What was your explanation for that quality (you recorded it above)? Sharing God's heart involves sharing his truth. How committed are you to sharing God's truths accurately and standing firm against teachings that distort his message and truths?*

Talking It Out

1. Given what you now know about elders and overseers in the first century, what church leadership positions or roles carried out in the twenty-first century do you see as comparable to what elders did in the first century? What about the first-century roles of overseers? What contemporary church leadership positions or roles do you think are closest to that of ancient overseers?

2. Do the church leaders you know (regardless of their titles or roles) live up to the biblical standards laid out in Titus 1:5–9? Should they? Take some time to discuss your answers.

3. It's fair to say that family life is the first place where leadership is tested. And even if you don't have a family, at one point you were part of one. Maybe you had to lead your siblings, or maybe you simply experienced being led by a parental figure. A leader's ability to manage a family and lead his or her children according to biblical principles is a reflection of his or her capacity to lead. Discuss your experience with leadership in your home growing up or your current family. What were or are the successes? What were or are the struggles?

4. Proverbs 15:1 says, "Respond gently when you are confronted." In Titus 1:9, Paul exhorted Titus to make certain that the leaders he appointed were able to "provide convincing answers" to those who might oppose them. Paul stopped short of giving instruction about the style of engagement, but given the various qualities he listed, discuss how responding with gentleness reflects Paul's qualifications for church leaders. Do you think that there might be an occasion where a gentle answer might not be appropriate? If so, when would that be?

LESSON 3

Shepherds and Liars

(Titus 1:10–16)

Perhaps the most popular psalm in the Bible is Psalm 23. Here are the first four verses in a translation that should be quite familiar to those of you who studied the Bible prior to the release of TPT (in fact, you likely have the introduction to Psalm 23 memorized):

> The LORD is my shepherd; I shall not want.
> He makes me lie down in green pastures.
> He leads me beside still waters.
> He restores my soul.
> He leads me in paths of righteousness
> for his name's sake.
> Even though I walk through the valley of
> the shadow of death,
> I will fear no evil,
> for you are with me;
> your rod and your staff,
> they comfort me (vv. 1–4 ESV).

The important, relevant verse when talking about false teaching (the topic of Titus 1:10–16) comes in the second part of Psalm 23:4, which TPT translates as the following: "Your authority is my strength and my peace." David, the author of Psalm 23, was a shepherd before he became a king. And that's why this particular psalm is so endearing. It's packed with illustrations related to David's shepherding work.

Two essential tools for shepherds in the ancient world were the rod and the staff, both mentioned in Psalm 23:4. Shepherds used the *rod* (a sturdy wooden stick) as both a weapon against wild animals and a device to count their sheep, also checking the grain of the sheep's wool as it passed under the rod, a process referenced in Leviticus 27:32, "And every tithe of herds and flocks, every tenth animal of all that pass under the herdsman's staff, shall be holy to the Lord" (ESV).[13] The other tool, the *staff,* was a longer, more slender stick, which often had a hooked end. Shepherds used it to direct the movement of the sheep and to save them from predators and sometimes from themselves.[14] For example, a sheep would sometimes get trapped or begin to wander off. In such a case, the shepherd could loop the curved end of the staff around the sheep's neck, redirecting and saving it.

- *Read Titus 1:10–16 and think about Psalm 23 and Paul's establishment of elders in Crete under the guidance of Titus. How would the host leaders in each local church be like shepherds, especially in the context of these verses from Titus?*

- *What shepherding role(s) do you think the elders would perform as they oversaw the numerous churches under their care?*

- *Think about the illustration of the Lord as your shepherd in Psalm 23. Jesus instructed Peter, in John 21:15–17, to "take care of my lambs." And Paul exhorted the elders of the church of Ephesus to act as "true shepherds over all the flock and feed them well" (Acts 20:28). How has the Lord been like a shepherd to you in your life?*

- *How have church leaders served in a similar capacity, leading you, guarding you, and (spiritually) feeding you?*

Facing False Teachers

- *Work back through Titus 1:10–16. What is Paul's description of the false teachers? What are their character traits and behaviors?*

- *What problems were these false teachers creating for Christians on the island of Crete?*

- *What advice did Paul give to Titus on how to handle these false teachers?*

- *What problems have you faced dealing with people who are untrustworthy, deceptive, and dishonest?*

- *What advice would you offer to fellow Christians who are facing such individuals and the problems they foster?*

THE BACKSTORY

When Paul referenced the issue of false teachers in Crete, he quoted from a Cretan writer named Epimenides. This man was a native of Crete who lived in the sixth century BC. The ancients described him as "a poet, a priest, and a prophet," and he was highly revered.[15] Paul quoted the pagan Epimenides as writing, "Those Cretans are nothing but liars, worthless beasts and lazy gluttons." That was quite an indictment—and one that Paul agreed with (vv. 12–13).

Was this assessment of the Cretans common in Paul's day? Apparently so.

> The Roman historian Titus Livius speaks of Cretan "avarice." The Greek historian Polybius writes of their "ferocity and fraud" and "their mendacity"—which could be called second-century BC political correctness. "Ferocity and fraud" and "mendacity" simply mean that Polybius thought Cretans were fierce, lying cheats. Another Greek historian, Diodorus Siculus, writes that the Cretans tend to "riotous insubordination." In *Halley's Bible Handbook*, Henry Halley comments that they were "bold sailors and great bowmen with loose morals."[16]

Bible commentator D. Edmond Hiebert pointed out that "the falsehood of the Cretans was proverbial. The expression 'to Cretize' meant 'to lie,' and 'to play the Cretan with a Cretan' meant 'to out-trick a trickster.'"[17] The Cretans had a reputation, and it wasn't a good one. And since Paul quoted from a Cretan who was also esteemed as a prophet, he put his readers on the horns of a dilemma. If they denied what their own prophet had said, then they would be saying that his words were false. But if they agreed with him, then they would be accepting his indictment of them, which was far from flattering.

Now, Paul's agreement with Epimenides does not mean that Paul believed that all Cretans—without exception—could be described as liars. For that would commit Paul to a paradox: If all Cretans are liars, then the Cretan Epimenides is a liar. If Epimenides is a liar, then his statement that "all Cretans are liars" is probably a lie. Thus, it wouldn't be true that "all Cretans are liars," and at least some Cretans tell the truth. This leads to a paradox: "All Cretans are liars" would be both true and false.

Along with this paradox, Paul would then be indicting even Cretan Christians as liars, which is highly unlikely. It's far more likely that Paul would have assumed that individuals eternally changed by faith in Christ would, on the whole, become truth-tellers. Lies would characterize them less and less as they matured in Christ through the transforming work of the Spirit.

The clue for how to interpret Paul's acceptance of the words of Epimenides is the immediate context in which he cited them. Paul placed the indictment of Cretans in the middle of his description of the false teachers. In other words, what Epimenides said about Cretans in general perfectly fit the character and behavior of the false teachers who were undermining families and turning people away from the truth and toward myths (vv. 11, 14). The false teachers, then, exhibited in abundance what the general reputation of the Cretans had become.

While the Cretans were regarded as morally corrupt in Paul's day, they had some merits in other respects. For instance, at least fifteen cities on the island prospered in the first century, "oil and wine production increased massively, amphitheaters, temples, Roman baths and aqueducts were built, and the island minted its own coinage. The famed Cretan archers became an important fixture in the Roman army across the empire."[18] The island's archers had even served as mercenaries as far back as the days of Alexander the Great during the 300s BC.[19]

Given what we know about first-century Crete, it's safe to say that church planting there wasn't easy. And the job of bringing order to churches in that culture had to be a struggle.

- *Have you ever tried to stand for the truth in the midst of a hostile environment? Describe the situation and the result.*

- *What was Paul's advice to Titus given the Cretan reputation (vv. 11, 13–14)?*

- *How can Paul's advice to Titus help you maintain vigilance in your Christian beliefs and practice, especially if you are trying to "correct [individuals] thoroughly so that their lives will line up with the truths of our faith" (v. 13)?*

EXPERIENCE GOD'S HEART

God's heart for you to maintain holiness, especially in the presence of false teaching, is very evident in this part of Titus. Paul wrote this in verse 15: "It's true that all is pure to those who have pure hearts, but to the corrupt unbelievers nothing is pure. Their minds and consciences are defiled."

- *How can modeling your life according to verses 6–9 prepare you more fully for times when you might be confronted by those Paul described in verses 10–16?*

- *Read 1 Timothy 4:1–7. There are several parallels to what Titus had to confront in Crete. Paul's solution for Titus on Crete was rooted in maintaining pureness of heart. What was his strategy for Timothy in Ephesus (see 1 Timothy 4:4–6 in particular)?*

- *Think of a situation where you had to confront a false teaching or even a liar. Maybe the situation didn't even have to do with a biblical truth or situation. Maybe you simply had to defend yourself or someone else from someone speaking against you. What was the situation, and how did you confront the individual(s)?*

- *Now, think about that situation you just described. Given what you've read in 1 Timothy 4 and Titus 1:10–16, could you have approached the situation differently? How can Paul's advice to both Titus and Timothy serve you in the future, in case you find yourself in a similar situation?*

SHARE GOD'S HEART

- *How does the idea of being "defiled" (v. 15) relate to sharing God's heart, especially today in a world where there is a good deal of spiritual confusion and false doctrine, just as there was in Titus' day on the island of Crete?*

- *How does sharing God's heart include both holding fast to truth as well as extending grace to those who are deceived?*

Talking It Out

1. Reread Titus 1:15–16. What does it mean for a person to be "disqualified from doing anything good"? What steps can you take to protect yourself from becoming disqualified by immoral behavior or, in the case of verses 10–16, false teaching?

2. Do you ever struggle to live out your Christian life in a way that authentically reflects your profession of faith? Why or why not?

3. How can you encourage your Christian brothers and sisters to better align their actions with Christian belief? In what ways do the verses that are the focus of this lesson encourage you to better align your beliefs with your actions, in particular as a reflection of God's heart for holiness?

4. How can the church of today seek to improve how it lives out the principles found in verses 10–16, especially in the context of confronting false teaching?

LESSON 4

Sound Doctrine + Godly Character = Disciples of Jesus

(Titus 2:1–6)

Pastor of Life.Church and author of numerous books, including *Altar Ego: Becoming Who God Says You Are*, Craig Groeschel has a large social media following (nearly three million and counting) and is known for many quotes. One of his more well-known is the following:

> As you'll recall, what you believe—about who you are and who God is—determines how you behave. If you believe everybody is going to criticize you, you'll behave cautiously. If you believe you're probably going to fail, you're going to venture out tentatively. If, however, you believe that the one true Lord God is calling you, empowering you, leading you, and equipping you, then you will live boldly. Why? Because boldness is behavior born of belief.[20]

Paul reminded Titus of this very concept in 2:1–6, instructing Titus to make the teaching of sound doctrine a priority. Why? So that the Christian church on Crete would be able to more fully represent and live out the gospel message. This is the essence of Christian discipleship, and it is what Jesus commanded his followers to do when he said, "Make disciples of all nations" (Matthew 28:19).

- *Before we go any further, read Titus 2:1–6. Jot down below what stands out to you in these verses.*

Paul's basic formula for creating disciples of Jesus is broad, though very evident in the first verse of Titus 2. For Paul, Christians make disciples when converts are taught to "embrace a lifestyle that is consistent with sound doctrine." It's really a great formula. And it makes sense that the teaching of sound doctrine will lead to increased godly character, which, in turn, will lead to more and more followers of Jesus.

- *Reread Groeschel's quote. What are your most basic beliefs about God?*

- *What are your most basic beliefs about who you are and how God sees you and works in you?*

- *When you consider the nature of God and how he truly sees you (as a redeemed son or daughter), how can your study of God's Word encourage you on a daily basis?*

- *Why does it matter that our lifestyle fits well with sound Christian doctrine?*

WORD WEALTH

What does Paul mean, exactly, when he told Titus to teach a lifestyle that is consistent with "sound doctrine"? Taking a look at the original Greek text reveals that "sound doctrine" is translated from two Greek words: *hugiano* and *didaskalia*, which can also be understood as "healthy teaching."[21]

The false teachers rejected what was true and replaced it with myths (1:14). They used this teaching to enrich themselves (v. 11) as they disrupted families and showed in their own lifestyles that they denied the true God (v. 16). In contrast, Paul called on Titus to teach the Christians in Crete to live in a manner consistent with true Christian doctrine (2:1). Their life choices needed to fit well with what Christianity actually taught, with what both Scripture and the apostles taught was true. This instruction was healthy; it brought wholeness as it honored human bodies and souls, seeing them in the light of the one true God who made humans his image-bearers and who provided them with a Savior who would restore and transform them into the fullness of what they were created to be and do.

- *What are your main sources for sound doctrine?*

- *How should church leaders (like Titus) model sound doctrine? How can church leaders encourage others to uphold sound doctrine and exhibit it in their lifestyles?*

Different Age Groups Within the Church

As Paul described what he wanted Titus to teach, he kept the details brief and general. But he also addressed four specific groups: male elders (older men), female elders (older women), younger women, and younger men. The use of the term "elders" here has nothing to do with the church office of elder. Instead it designates the more elderly age group of men and women.

Older Men

- *Read Titus 2:2. What did Paul want Titus to lead the older men in the Cretan churches to do?*

- *Recalling the cultural moral degradation on Crete at the time, what influence would you imagine that older men living according to Paul's counsel would have on their families, friends, neighbors, business associates, and even governing authorities? (In the ancient world, older men and women were generally respected, honored, and often consulted for the wisdom they had accumulated over their lifetime.)*

- *Are there any male figures in your life that exhibit at least some of the traits mentioned in verse 2? If so, who are they, and what influence have they had on your life?*

- *What do you consider to be a disciplined life? Is self-discipline a characteristic of your life? Why or why not?*

- *Self-control was one of Paul's favorite character traits. He used it when he described the qualities of overseers (1:8) and when he provided advice for younger women (2:5). Why is self-control such an important quality for a Christian and especially for a Christian leader?*

Older Women

- *Now read what Paul wanted Titus to help elderly women to do on Crete (Titus 2:3). How did Paul want the older women to live?*

- *What insight does Paul's counsel give you into the lifestyle choices of older Cretan women in his day?*

- *In verse 4, Paul noted what this course correction for elderly women would enable them to do. What task would they then be able to perform much better and for whose benefit?*

- *Is there an older woman in your life who lives according to the Christian faith? If so, who is it, and what influence has she had on your life?*

- *Given the context of verse 3, what do you think it means to be a teacher of "beautiful things"?*

Younger Women

- *Read Titus 2:4–5. Note that Paul did not ask Titus to lead the young women. Instead, he thought that if Titus could get the older women to live the Christian life more consistently and to embrace their role as teachers, those older women would be the ones who would "teach the younger women" how they needed to live. What, then, did Paul want the older women to teach the younger women? How did he want the younger women to live?*

- *Have you ever been mentored in the Christian faith? If so, describe that experience and its effectiveness.*

- *Why do you think Paul talked about older women teaching younger women how to love their families? Do you think love needs to be taught? Does all love come naturally? Is it a natural human inclination to show generous, other-centered love?*

- *Can you think of a recent example where you felt that you had a difficult time showing the love of God to a family member? What biblical principles helped you through the difficulty? Were those principles taught to you, were they demonstrated to you by a parent or mentor, or was it some combination of both teaching and example?*

- *How do self-control and purity go together (v. 5)?*

- *What were young women expected to take care of and be devoted to (v. 5)?*

- *Assuming the young women did all that Paul desired, what would that achieve (v. 5)? Why would that matter given what you know about first-century Crete?*

- *Do you think that living more in line with biblical teaching would have the same result in our day, whether you are male or female? Why or why not?*

THE BACKSTORY

Paul wanted the younger women to take "care of their household" (v. 5). This was a critically important task. In the ancient world, the household was so important that it was widely considered foundational to the health of the city-state. Even "secular ethicists saw the stability of the city-state as dependent upon responsible management of the household."[22] Along with the immediate family, a household "typically extended to include slaves, freedmen, servants and laborers, and sometimes even business associates and tenants."[23] For Paul, then, to call on the younger women to manage their households well meant that they needed to take charge of the people under their care, which would include handling conflicts, ordering a wide variety of activities, ensuring a host of needs were met daily, and participating in the maintenance and advancement of the family business. If a woman ran the household well, she created a place that "provided members with a sense of security and identity that the larger political and social structures were unable to give."[24]

Younger Men

Paul ended this section of his letter to Titus by focusing on younger men, and he kept it brief: "Likewise, guide the younger men into living disciplined lives for Christ" (v. 6). Here, Paul evoked what he previously said about older men and women as well as younger women, since a disciplined life certainly encompasses all his previous counsel.

- *Similar to how Paul generalized his ideas for teaching the Christian male and female elders in Crete and the younger women in the church, why do you think that Paul didn't provide any specifics for how to train up the younger men?*

- *When it came to the situation on the island of Crete, was Paul more concerned with method (how to make disciples) or character (how disciples should be and live) when it came to discipleship? Support your answer from the first chapters of Titus.*

EXPERIENCE GOD'S HEART

In Titus 2:1–6, Paul instructed Titus to teach the various age groups to seek godliness by refining their character and striving for more disciplined lives.

- *When considering Paul's instructions to Titus, what do you see as God's heart for the older generation in the church?*

- *What do you see as God's desire for the younger generation given what Paul advised?*

- *To which generation do you belong? How does Paul's counsel for your age group fit with your situation?*

SHARE GOD'S HEART

- *Paul told Titus that he had a "duty…to teach" the Cretan believers "to embrace a lifestyle that is consistent with sound doctrine" (v. 1). Has God called you to teach or to pass along God's heart for others in a different way? If so, what would you say your calling is? How are you practicing it?*

- *How does teaching grounded in sound doctrine encourage you to orient your character and actions around that teaching?*

- *What can you do to pass along Christian truths so as to influence others to live out those truths?*

Talking It Out

1. If you are part of the younger generation of believers, do you seek to learn what the older Christians can teach you? If so, discuss how you do this. If you don't strive to learn from older believers, why is this so? What is holding you back?

2. If you are an older-generation Christian, what are you doing to pass along to younger believers what you have learned? And if you are not doing this, why not?

3. In what aspect(s) of living a more disciplined life do you need to grow the most? (Identifying a few of these areas can help cause you to improve, letting you become more like Jesus and simultaneously stirring up others to live a more sanctified life and hopefully become a Christian if they aren't already.)

4. Why is the emphasis on sound doctrine and living in accordance with that doctrine so significant for the church's testimony in the world? Put another way, why is it important that Christians live according to what they say they believe?

LESSON 5

Service From the Top Down

(Titus 2:7–10)

Titus' work as a church leader under the apostle Paul was an act of service. He had assisted Paul for a long time and in a number of ways. In the process, Titus had proved himself to be "an ideal pastor."[25] For instance, in 2 Corinthians,

> Paul reflects very favorably upon Titus' genuine devotion and pastoral concern (2 Cor 8:16, 17). His earnestness is mentioned as a challenge to the Corinthians. Titus' joy and devoted concern was an inspiration to Paul in his reconciliation with the Corinthians (7:13–15). Paul substantiates his devotion to the Corinthians by arguing that he was of the same mind and attitude as Titus (12:18). These scattered allusions to the character of Titus indicate his close relationship to Paul and stellar qualifications as a pastor.[26]

In his character, behavior, and service, Titus exhibited what Jesus wanted to be marks of all of his disciples.

Fundamentally, a disciple is a student. And Jesus noted, "Students are not greater than their teacher. But the student who is fully trained will become like the teacher" (Luke 6:40 NLT). As Christ's disciples, we need to imitate him, to be like him, to follow his example. Jesus said as much when, after washing the feet of his disciples, he told them: "You've called me your teacher and lord, and you're right, for that's who I am. So if I'm your teacher and lord and have just washed your dirty feet, then you should follow the example that I've set for you.…A servant is not superior to his master, and an apostle is never greater than the one who sent him" (John 13:13–16). All of us—no matter our ethnicity, age, social standing, marital status, talents, or calling—are students of Jesus Christ, the master Teacher and our Lord. Our learning from him involves our service to him. And that service is to be carried out by serving others, especially those who are in God's household, the church.

Paul and Titus were both students of Jesus, both imitating and serving him. And Titus served under Paul's direction, advancing Paul's ministry, just as Jesus served under the Father and carried out his will (John 4:34; 5:19; 6:38). Titus was a true disciple of Jesus, imitating and serving the Savior under the apostle Paul.

Servants All

- *Read Titus 2:7–10. Write below what stands out to you in those verses.*

In Titus 2:7–8, Paul gave his protégé more direction for his service on Crete. Then Paul moved from his chosen leader on the island to a class of persons who were among the lowest on the social strata in the Roman Empire—slaves (vv. 9–10). And yet, from the top of the church to the bottom, Paul regarded all persons as equal followers of Jesus Christ. As Paul said in his letter to the Galatians, "We no longer see each other in our former state—Jew or non-Jew, enslaved or free,[27] male or female—because we're all one through our union with Jesus Christ" (3:28).

To the Church Leader Titus

- *Reread Titus 2:7–8. What was the first thing Paul urged Titus to do in these verses?*

- *What kind of life was Titus to live and why? What did his role as teacher have to do with all of it?*

- *What is the value in demonstrating integrity in all that one teaches? What does that even mean (v. 7; see the TPT footnote on the verse)?*

- *What impact would Titus' life have on critics, assuming he lived as Paul advised (v. 8)?*

- *Have you observed that a noble, high-integrity life can still garner criticism, unwarranted though it may be? Why do you think this happens?*

- *Unjustified criticism, while sometimes difficult to handle, can bring a cost to accusers. Paul mentioned the cost of embarrassment (v. 8). What other costs could be experienced by those who charge Christians falsely or unfairly?*

- *Did you notice that Paul wanted Titus to see his life as "a model" for others (v. 7)? Are you living in such a way that others would want to pattern at least aspects of their lives after yours? What do you think is admirable in your life? You may want to ask someone close to you what they find worth imitating in your life. This is an opportunity for you to learn how you are perceived and why.*

To Christian Slaves

In verse 9, the reference to "servants" denotes slaves or bond-servants.[28] In the ancient world, slavery was common, and in the Roman Empire, it's estimated that enslaved individuals and families made up a quarter to a third of the population of Italy.[29] Outside of Italy, the number of slaves varied widely, with some regions of the empire having far fewer than others.[30] (You'll find more information about slavery in the lessons on the letter of Philemon.)

One thing we learn from the New Testament is that some Christians were slaves. And on the island of Crete, there were enough Christian slaves in the churches for Paul to provide Titus guidance on instructing them.

- *Read through Titus 2:9–10. How did Paul want slaves to relate to their masters (v. 9)?*

- *What does it mean to you to be "pleasing in every way" (v. 9)?*

- *What were slaves not to do (vv. 9–10; see footnote 'g' for verse 10)?*

- *Why would the absence of such behaviors be important in a master-slave relationship?*

- *What were slaves supposed to prove to their masters and why (v. 10)?*

THE BACKSTORY

Slaves in the Roman Empire were mostly foreigners (that is, not from Italy or Greece). They may have become slaves as prisoners of war or as captives of pirates. Abandoned infants could be taken and raised as slaves. Sometimes parents sold their children into slavery to pay off debts or stave off poverty. Some individuals condemned as criminals could become part of the slave population.[31] One scholar pointed out that individuals sometimes "sold themselves [into slavery] to pay debts, to escape poverty, to climb socially or to obtain special governmental positions."[32]

Slavery in the Roman Empire had nothing to do with ethnicity, racial bigotry, or even a desire to see people suffer. Instead, slavery was an "'institutionalized system of large-scale employment.'"[33] Some slaves served as farm workers, miners, or builders. Educated slaves practiced as "doctors, architects, and teachers."[34] Slaves could also be found working as servants in private residences and helping their masters manage their businesses and even maintain the books of those businesses.[35] Most slaves were much better off socioeconomically than the poor. "Free and impoverished persons who had to seek work each day without any certainty of employment occupied the lowest level" of society. "Some of them sold themselves into slavery in order to obtain job security, food, clothing and shelter."[36] Some slaves made so much money over time that they could own their own property and even their own slaves. Many slaves earned enough money to purchase their own freedom.

Slaves who had been granted freedom by their owners, managed to purchase their own freedom, or even were bought by another person who then set them free were called freedmen. Once free, they could become Roman citizens, but they remained ineligible for political office. But even this restriction had exceptions. One notable example is the Roman governor Marcus Antonius Felix, mentioned in Acts 23–25. He "had been a slave until Antonia, the emperor Claudius's mother, manumitted him."[37]

While some slaves working on agricultural estates were

chained, "working in gangs in the fields in the daytime and locked in prisons at night,"[38] many others had freedom of movement, some even traveling for and with their masters. It must have been slaves who could move around who attended local gatherings of Christians. They could meet and worship with believers, perhaps also attending with their masters. These probably were the slaves who at least initially heard Paul's counsel coming through Titus and other church leaders.

- *The New Testament writers used the common practice of slavery to convey essential truths about our relationship to sin, self, other people, and God. Look up each of the following passages, and then next to each one write down how slavery is used to communicate truths about our spiritual condition and relationships. (Note that the Greek word for slave is doulos, often translated "servant," "love-servant," "loving servant," or even "employee" in TPT).*

    John 8:34–36

    John 15:15 (see footnote 'a' for this verse)

    Romans 6:16–20 ("servant" means "slave" in this context)

1 Corinthians 7:20–24

1 Corinthians 9:19–21

2 Corinthians 4:5

Galatians 4:1–9

He Became a Slave for Us

God's ultimate identification with us came through his Son, Jesus. As Paul put it, "He [God the Son] existed in the form of God, yet he gave no thought to seizing equality with God as his supreme prize. Instead he emptied himself of his outward glory by reducing himself to the form of a lowly servant"—that is, a *doulos*, a slave (Philippians 2:6–7). And what was this slave form? The Son "became human! He humbled himself and became vulnerable, choosing to be revealed as a man and was obedient" (vv. 7–8). Bible scholar R. Tuente brings out some of the fullness of the Son's incarnation when he writes:

> When Christ takes on the form of a slave, he enters into full solidarity with mankind in its subjection to sin, law and death. As servant, he is subject to the *nomos* [law] (Gal. 4:4) and bears its curse (Gal. 3:13). He takes on a form "that was like that of sinful flesh" (Rom. 8:3), and thus made himself a brother of men "who through fear of death must serve in bondage all their lives long" (Heb. 2:15). It is the form of the servant that exactly describes Jesus Christ's incarnation as the deepest self-abasement.[39]

The Son became one of us in order to show us God, to love us as God does, to minister among us, and to take our judgment upon himself so we could be set free from slavery to sin, the law, and death, and live an everlasting life in service of the ultimate good—God himself.

EXPERIENCE GOD'S HEART

- *Have you yielded your life to God through Jesus his Son? Or are you still under the control of sin, the law, and death? Through the Son you can find freedom because he has paid the price you owe. Just put your trust (faith) in him as your Savior and Lord. Confess your sins to him and receive him into your life.*

- *If you are already a freed man or woman in Christ, take time now to express your deep gratitude for his manumission. Praise him! Honor him. Worship him.*

SHARE GOD'S HEART

- *What do you see as the relationship between living a godly life and being a vocal witness for the gospel? What is your personal experience living out those two aspects of the Christian life?*

Talking It Out

1. It's important for a Christian worker to be known as dependable and faithful. And as a Christian in general, you want to be known as someone whom others can rely on. Imagine the extent to which a servant/slave would have stood out on the island of Crete in the AD 60s if they took Paul's advice to heart after converting to Christianity. What are the qualities of a loyal and trustworthy employee? Would you consider yourself to be such an employee? Why or why not?

2. What's the difference between being argumentative and giving arguments and reasons for the truth of the Christian faith? From what you've learned so far in your study of the letter to Titus, what would you say Paul wanted Titus to do in his ministry to the churches on Crete?

3. Have you ever had to deal with an argumentative person? How did you handle that? How effective was your approach? Why is it difficult to deal with such a person?

4. Given what you've learned about slavery in the Roman Empire, how does it compare to slavery in the history of your country? Do you believe that slavery should be a common human practice? Why or why not?

LESSON 6

Marked and Motivated by Grace

(Titus 2:11–15)

An infant has clothes and food. Yes, the infant needs these things, but the infant has done nothing to earn them. They are given because someone has shown favor to the child.

A homeless woman receives care from a passerby who asks for nothing in return—just gives to someone in need. The care has not been earned, but it has been given—and received—nonetheless.

A teenager receives an all-expenses-paid trip overseas. He did not work for it, but his parents gave it to him because they loved him and thought it would benefit him in several ways.

All of these examples exhibit what the Bible calls grace. Grace is unmerited favor. It is not something we earn. We can't get it by working for it, and it's not given to us because we deserve it. It's provided because someone cares enough to offer it.[40]

Titus 2:11–15 centers on God's grace and that it has been granted to us. We didn't earn it, and we certainly don't deserve it. But God, out of the unlimited abundance of his love and mercy, has offered his unmerited favor to human beings. Now the questions are twofold: Will we receive it, and what will we do with it?

- *Before we dive into the details of this section of Titus, read through 2:11–15. Jot down here what stands out to you in these verses.*

God's Grace to Us

- *Reread verse 11. How was God's grace manifested? And what did this grace provide and to whom?*

- *Now turn to Ephesians 2:8–9. What do these verses add to your understanding of God's grace and the gift that came through it?*

- *What is the proper response to receiving a gift? When someone gives you a gift, how do you respond? Do you remember what it was like when you were a child and got the "best gift ever"? How did you feel and respond then?*

- *Return to Titus 2 and read verses 13–14. Who gave himself for our salvation, and what did his life purchase?*

DIGGING DEEPER

Did you notice that Paul called Jesus "our great God and Savior" (v. 13)? The biblical witness is that Jesus was God. The apostle Peter affirmed this, calling Jesus "our God and Savior" (2 Peter 1:1), as does the apostle John, referring to Jesus as "God's Son…the true God and eternal life" (1 John 5:20). At the start of his gospel, John referred to Jesus as "the Living Expression" who was "fully God" (1:1). And the apostle Paul, in his first letter to the Corinthians, called Jesus "Lord" and added that it is through him that "we and all things exist" (8:6)—an activity only God can perform.

Now, these Christ followers were only affirming what Jesus

said of himself. During his ministry, Jesus told the Jewish leaders that God was his Father and that he was working along with the Father. For this, these leaders wanted to kill Jesus because he was claiming that he was "equal to God" (John 5:17–18). On yet another occasion, Jesus told Jewish leaders that "the Father and I are one" (10:30). This so enraged these leaders that "they picked up rocks to stone him to death" (v. 31). Why? Because they charged him with blasphemy for claiming "to be God," though he was supposedly just a man (v. 33). During a testy confrontation with many Jewish leaders, Jesus confirmed that he had not only seen Abraham, their founding father of old, but he preexisted Abraham! Said Jesus, "I give you this eternal truth: I have existed long before Abraham was born, for I AM!" (8:57–58). By declaring his identity to be I AM, Jesus named himself to be the very one who spoke to Moses out of the burning bush and revealed his name to be I AM (Exodus 3:13–14). Jesus was YAHWEH—the eternal, immortal, indestructible, all-powerful, all-knowing God of the universe.

Jesus not only declared his deity but proved it. For instance, Jesus forgave sins directly and personally, an action reserved for a holy, righteous, and just God (Mark 2:5–12; cf. Isaiah 43:25, 27). Jesus also accepted worship, an action reserved for God alone (Matthew 14:33; 28:9; Luke 5:8; 24:52; cf. Exodus 34:14). Jesus performed countless miracles, indicating that God was authenticating and approving of his teaching and actions, which included Jesus' claims to being God and possessing the prerogatives and abilities of God (John 5:17–29, 39–40; 6:38–40; 10:36–38). And Jesus raised himself from the dead, an action only God, the giver of life, could do (John 2:18–22; cf. Matthew 27:62–63; 28:6; Luke 24:6–7).

Along with being God, Jesus was also human. He was one of King David's descendants (Matthew 1:1; Luke 1:32; Romans 1:3) and born of a woman (Matthew 1:18–25; Luke 2:1–7; Galatians 4:4). He grew intellectually and physically (Luke 2:40, 52). He became hungry (Matthew 4:2; Mark 11:12) and tired (Luke 8:23). He prayed, showing his dependence on the Father and the Spirit (Matthew 14:23; Mark 1:35; 14:32–40; John 17; Hebrews 5:7), received angelic support (Mark 1:13), and could be subject to temptation (though he never sinned; see Matthew 4:1–11; 2 Corinthians 5:21; Hebrews 2:18; 4:15; 1 John 3:5). He had to travel to get from one place to another (see all four Gospels), and he died with his human body fixed to a cross (Matthew 27:35, 50; Mark 15:37, 39, 44–45; Luke 23:33, 46; John 19:18, 30, 33–34; Hebrews 2:14; cf. Isaiah 53:8–9, 12).

So Jesus was God and man at the same time. Reflection on such passages eventually led the church to articulate these truths this way: Jesus was fully divine in one nature and fully human in another nature, with both natures conjoined or united (not separated or mixed together) in one divine person, the Son of God.[41] So Jesus suffered fatigue, hunger, and death in his human nature, not in his divine nature.[42] What is proper for humanity was also true of *his* humanity. What Jesus did not experience, however, was giving in to temptation and sinning. While he still had to deal with being tempted, he never surrendered to it—he always won over it. In fact, he could say that he always did what the Father wanted him to do (John 5:19, 30; 8:28–29). Jesus was obedient, even unto death (Philippians 2:8).

Moreover, Jesus' human nature from his conception was like Adam and Eve's before they sinned—uncorrupted. Jesus' human nature was created all good by the Holy Spirit in the womb of Mary the virgin (Matthew 1:18, 20–21; Luke 1:34–35). This is how human beings were originally created—good, lacking any corruption whatsoever (Genesis 1:26–27, 31). But all of this changed for humanity with the sin of Adam and Eve (Genesis 3; Romans 5:12–19). Jesus was like the first human couple, except when temptation came his way, he remained faithful to the Father and never rebelled.

The Life of Grace

- *Returning to Titus 2, look again at verse 14. What does Christ save us from? And what does he save us to become?*

- *For Christians to become pure, we have a role to play. Look at verse 12. What are we supposed to turn from?*

- *In what ways has God's grace taught you to reject sin?*

- *In that same verse, what are supposed to turn toward—that is, how are we to live now that we have been saved by grace?*

- *How does God's saving grace motivate you to be holy?*

- *This grace-centered life includes our waiting patiently for something yet to come (v. 13). What is this future event?*

- *Do you personally long for Christ's second coming? Why or why not?*

Truth-Centered Service

Paul ended Titus 2 with an admonition to his ministry partner Titus. Paul wanted him to take four actions. Let's take a look at each one.

- *The first action was to preach (v. 15). What was to be the content of Titus' preaching?*

- *The second action was to exhort (v. 15). Who was he to exhort, and what was he to exhort them to do?*

- *The third action was to expose a certain thing (v. 15). What was Titus supposed to expose, and why was he told to do this?*

- *The fourth action concerned something Titus was told to not allow to affect him (v. 15). What was that?*

- *What are three truths you have found to be essential to living a grace-filled life?*

- *Do you exhort other people to follow these truths? If so, what does your exhortation look like, and how effective is it?*

- *Are you willing to expose sin in another person's life and help them correct the problem? If you have done that, what happened, and what did you learn from the encounter?*

- *Have you ever been intimidated into silence rather than communicating your Christian convictions or shrunk back behind closed doors rather than living out your faith publicly? If so, what happened? Why were you fearful?*

- *Have you gained the needed courage to speak about your faith and live it out before others? If so, how did that occur for you?*

- *What is your experience with holding other Christians accountable to biblical standards? Does holding others accountable come naturally to you? Why or why not?*

EXPERIENCE GOD'S HEART

- *Why did Jesus die for you? How does that make you feel? What does that lead you to want to do for him?*

- *In verse 11, Paul said that God's grace brings the news of salvation to all people. What do you see as God's heart for all people, regardless of their past or current situation? What does your view say about God's desire to redeem everyone?*

- *How is God training you through his grace? Are there areas of your life where you feel God challenging you to renounce worldly passions or ungodliness? How does God's grace help you in this process?*

SHARE GOD'S HEART

- *How can you better bring the message of God's gracious salvation to those individuals in your circles of influence who need it?*

- *What does living a godly life have to do with reflecting God's heart in your interactions with others?*

- *What do you believe is your role in teaching and correcting others?*

Talking It Out

1. What makes Christ's second coming such a glorious event, something that gives Christians much anticipation and hope?

2. In verse 15, Paul instructed Titus to teach, encourage, and rebuke with authority. How should a Christian balance grace and truth when sharing God's heart with others? How does God's heart for discipline and instruction show up in how Christians should guide one another?

3. Christianity isn't passive; it's about being zealous for good deeds and working for God's kingdom. What do you do to make sure you are involved in the daily work of the gospel—caring and helping others, preaching the gospel, living a grace-filled life, etc.?

LESSON 7

Living Engaged, Living Transformed

(Titus 3:1–3)

Located in central Arkansas, Hot Springs Village is the largest gated community in North America.[43] Sitting at just over forty square miles and encompassing twenty-six thousand acres, you'd hardly know you were in a gated community—other than the fact that you have to pass through security and abide by all kinds of regulations and rules with which you might not otherwise be accustomed.

Have you ever lived in a gated community? Or maybe you know someone who does. Some people love it because it offers exclusive features and feelings of safety and privacy. For others, however, it makes them feel isolated and trapped.

- *Have you ever lived in a gated community or in an area governed by a homeowners' association? Do you live in an area where you see neighbors regularly? What is your experience trying to live as a Christian among your community and neighbors?*

At least one thing gated communities provide is a place where their residents can go to be quartered off from the rest of the world, to be separate and protected. The apostle Paul did not want fellow Christians to live that way, even on the island of Crete. They were not to steal themselves away into communities reserved only for Christians. He wanted them publicly visible and engaged in numerous ways. He desired that they

- *be known for their hospitality (Titus 1:8);*
- *be recognized as "fair-minded, pure-hearted, and self-controlled" (v. 9);*
- *challenge false teachers who were "disrupting entire families" (v. 11);*
- *if slaves, be "supportive of their masters" (2:9);*
- *realize, teach, and demonstrate that, in Christ, God has provided the way of salvation for everyone (vv. 11, 15).*

In Titus 3, Paul brought out some of the fuller implications of how Christians are to live in the public square. In doing so, he contrasted how believers had lived before they put their lives in the hands of Christ and his Spirit. The picture is sobering and instructive.

- *Read the first three verses of Titus 3 and then write below some of your observations about what Paul said here. Feel free to jot down any questions these verses raise too.*

THE BACKSTORY

For most of us, whether our home is a single-structure dwelling or a townhome or apartment, our private residence is just that—private. We can shut our front door and close the shades and become invisible to the outside world. This is normal for the vast majority of us. But this was not the case in the first-century world of the Roman Empire. While Greek-inspired housing tended to create privacy for residents, Roman houses did not. Romans made no distinction between a place of work and a place of leisure. The home was a workspace, a place of business. "Business was regularly conducted at home, whether by an emperor receiving the reports of his secretaries and procurators, by a republican noble giving his legal advice, or by a merchant, craftsman, or shopkeeper operating from the *officina* (workshop) or *taberna* (shop) that were part of the house."[44]

Like a place of business, the front door was usually open. And

> when a passerby looked through the open doors of these houses, he or she could see right through the house! Often a visual axis ran from the door through the atrium, then through the tablinum, that is, through the "living room/office" where the owner was displayed as if upon a stage (with the floor actually built a few inches higher than the other rooms), and then into the peristyle, the colonnaded garden.[45]

Dining areas, bathrooms (if there were any), and bedrooms could not be seen by passersby or even guests conducting business in the central places of the house. Still, much of a Roman house was open to the public.

Most people in the ancient world could not afford large houses. Apartment dwelling and living in small, closed-off rooms behind a small business were much more common. In fact, "the majority of urban dwellers lived in small, dark, poorly ventilated, crowded buildings where privacy was unavailable, adequate sanitation impossible, and the spread of disease inevitable."[46]

Still, privacy in the Roman Empire was hard to come by. And one's home did not automatically guarantee a place of privacy and refuge from the outside world.

Living Engaged

Given how people lived in first-century Crete, it was inevitable that most of their daily routines were in public view. Christians could have found private quarters in which to worship and to live out their beliefs secretly, as did members of the Mithras cult.[47] But Paul did not want Christ followers to be walled off from the world.

- *Read Titus 3:1. What two pieces of counsel did Paul want the Cretan believers to follow?*

- *Given what you have learned about Crete and its people during Paul's day, what kind of issues might the Christians have faced there as they tried to follow the apostle's guidance?*

- *Let's bring Paul's counsel into our day. Consider each of the phrases below. Then respond to each one, noting any difficulties or struggles you find following each one in your given situation.*

  Having "respect [for] governmental leaders"

  Being a "law-abiding" citizen

  Being "ready to fulfill" your "civic duty"

- *Let's go a bit deeper on these matters. Reflect on the questions that follow, answering them as well as you can with the biblical knowledge you now have. Also know that Christians have disagreed over some of the issues that these questions raise.*[48]

  Can a Christian show respect to a government leader while also disagreeing with that leader's policies, positions, and/or behavior? Explain your answer.

Should a Christian always abide by the laws of his or her country? Support your answer.

If a Christian's performance of his or her "civic duty" would violate biblical teaching, should he or she perform that duty? Support your answer.

Living Transformed

On the heels of Paul's counsel regarding how Christians should relate to government and society, Paul encouraged Titus to remind the Cretan Christians how they should be toward those individuals who cross their paths.

- *Reread verse 2 of chapter 3, then fill in the following blanks, noting the qualities that Paul called upon Christians to have as they interact with others. Then write down your own thoughts about Paul's counsel.*

"Never __________ __________ anyone with their words or __________." Personal thoughts:

"Instead be __________, __________, and __________ to everyone." Personal thoughts:

- *What did Paul want Christians to remember with regard to their lives before they knew God's grace (v. 3)?*

EXPERIENCE GOD'S HEART

Titus 3:1–3 certainly conveys that God has a heart for order and respect. He wants his people to live in harmony and peace and be the kind of people who are welcoming, not abrasive, disrespectful, or enslaved to their former way of life.

- *Are you the kind of citizen who represents Jesus Christ well? Why or why not?*

- *The footnote for Titus 3:2 states, "The implication is that we accept the differences of others and allow people to be who they are and not try to make them over into our image of who we think they should be." Restate this in your own words. Is this the way you treat others?*

SHARE GOD'S HEART

- *Given the need to spread the gospel, which was one of Paul's main goals, why would Paul advocate for respect and submission to the government and its leaders? Do you think such a practice would do more to promote or hinder the spread of the gospel? Explain your answer.*

- *How have you, as a Christian, "fulfill[ed your] civic duty" (v. 1)? What was your experience like? What were the results?*

- *What role does our speech play in demonstrating God's heart for others?*

Talking It Out

1. Do you know of anyone who has been persecuted by a governing authority for their Christian beliefs or practices? What happened? What were the results?

2. Do you think it is ever justified for Christians to disobey the laws of the land? Do your best to support your answer biblically.

3. What was your life like before you accepted God's grace in Christ? Now contrast that with what you are like today. What are some of the differences? Why might recalling them on occasion be helpful?

LESSON 8

Salvation in Song

(Titus 3:4–7)

When Paul wrote to the Christians in Ephesus, he told them, "Keep speaking to each other with words of Scripture, singing the Psalms with praises and spontaneous songs given by the Spirit!" (Ephesians 5:19). The early church was a singing church. And in the New Testament, we have at least snippets of some of these ancient hymns (e.g., Ephesians 5:14; Philippians 2:6–11; 2 Timothy 2:11–13).[49]

Well, many Bible scholars believe Titus 3:4–7 to be one of these early hymns.[50] And its focus—what it celebrates in song—is salvation in Christ as granted by God through his grace. As Paul exclaimed at the start of verse 8, the message of this hymn is "true and faithful."

- *Read this hymn in Titus 3:4–7. Summarize what you think it teaches about our salvation in Christ.*

Biblical Principles

Songs are better sung than analyzed, but we don't know the music that conveys the lyrics, and these lyrics are rich in content about salvation. So we are going to move through this ancient hymn to see what we can learn about God, his Son, and what he has granted us by his grace.

There are four overall themes we can glean from Titus 3:4–7. Let's call them biblical principles—concepts that were just as true for Titus and his church planting and organizing efforts in Crete as they are for all Christians. They are salvation by God's compassion, love, and mercy; the role of the Holy Spirit; inheritance; and the fullness of salvation.

1) Salvation by God's Compassion, Love, and Mercy

God's beautiful compassion, love, and mercy, which constitute his grace, are evident in this song.

- *Read Titus 3:4–7. Underline or highlight the occurrences of "compassion," "love," and "mercy." Then answer the following questions.*

    How are God's compassion and love described (vv. 4–5, 7)?

    In whom did they appear, and how obvious were they in him (vv. 4, 6)?

What outcome did God seek to achieve through his compassion, love, and mercy?

Has that outcome become real in your life? If so, how did it come about?

2) The Role of the Holy Spirit

The full Trinity is actually referenced in verses 4–6. God the Father is mentioned straight away in verse 4 as our loving, saving, compassionate God. Jesus, the Messiah, is mentioned as the source of life in verse 6. And the Holy Spirit's role in a Christian's salvation is also mentioned in verse 6.

- *Reread verse 6. What does it convey about the role of the Holy Spirit in salvation? What does he do for us?*

- *By making us "completely new" (v. 6), we are now what (v. 7)?*

To be faultless here does not mean to be sinless. As the hymn says, it means to be "innocent before his face" (v. 7). And whose face is that? The face of the triune God. In other words, in a judicial sense, we have been declared no longer guilty (Romans 3:23–28). This has set us free from the *penalty* of sin, which is death. This is what the *justification* aspect of salvation is all about. Our divine Judge accepts Jesus' payment on the cross for our sin. His death and resurrection canceled our debt and set us free (Colossians 2:12–14). As Paul said in Romans 5:1–2,

> Our faith in Jesus transfers God's righteousness to us and he now declares us flawless in his eyes. This means we can now enjoy true and lasting peace with God, all because of what our Lord Jesus, the Anointed One, has done for us. Our faith guarantees us permanent access into this marvelous kindness that has given us a perfect relationship with God.

However, sin can still exercise power over us if we let it. Our newness in Christ, which comes through the transforming work of the Holy Spirit, gives us a new start and new power. The Holy Spirit gives us the power we need to fight against sin and win (Romans 6:9–18). We will not always be victorious, and when we fail, we need to confess our sin knowing that our divine Savior will forgive us through the payment Christ has already provided for sin (1 John 1:8–2:2). This aspect of our lives is called *sanctification*, and it deals with delivering us from the *power* of sin in our lives. Through this process we are becoming more and more like Jesus, being conformed to his image. Paul put it this way in his letter to the Corinthians:

> We can all draw close to him [the Holy Spirit] with the veil removed from our faces. And with no veil we all become like mirrors who brightly reflect the glory of

> the Lord Jesus. We are being transfigured into his very image as we move from one brighter level of glory to another. And this glorious transfiguration comes from the Lord, who is the Spirit. (2 Corinthians 3:18)

3) Inheritance

- *Now justified by faith in Christ, his love gift to us is what (Titus 3:7)?*

- *Compare this love gift to what Jesus said in Matthew 5:5. What is our inheritance here, and how does it relate to what Paul said in Titus 3:7?*

- *Now add to all of this what the apostle John saw in a vision as recorded in Revelation 21:1–22:5. What does the "all things" of Titus 3:7 really include?*

Our future life will be one completely free of sin, including its very presence. This is the final phase of salvation—glorification.

4) The Fullness of Salvation

Titus 3:4–7 celebrates in song the comprehensive nature of salvation—it includes God's compassion and his desire to forgive sins and declare us judicially faultless (justification); the spiritual rebirth and transformation that comes from the Holy Spirit (sanctification); and the hope and inheritance we have of the fullness that eternal life in a new heavens and new earth will bring (glorification). Through Christ, our deliverance will be complete.

Human sin poses a problem that only God can solve. The hymn in Titus celebrates his comprehensive and glorious solution.

The song closes with the words "hope of eternal life" (v. 7). While we have eternal life now in Christ, it's also true that the full experience of that life is yet to come, for it will include a new world untainted by evil. This should encourage us to persevere through whatever we face on this side of that full life. What do you see as the relationship between hope and perseverance in the Christian life? How does your receipt of the fullness of salvation encourage you to continue to persevere?

EXPERIENCE GOD'S HEART

- *The hymn makes it clear that the salvation God brings is based on his mercy, not on our deeds (v. 5). Why can we not earn our way into God's favor?*

- *God's compassion, mercy, and love are expressions of his all-good nature. We can't receive them by demanding them, and we have not done anything to deserve them. If anything, we deserve condemnation and judgment (Romans 1–4). But God chose to reach out to us by his grace. Why do you think he has made this choice?*

- *God's mercy is the foundation of your salvation and anyone else's if they put their faith in Christ. What does this tell you about God's heart for the lost and the undeserving? How much does he really care about his human creatures?*

- *What does Titus 3:4–7 tell you about God's view of humanity's self-sufficient efforts to make their lives right? How does this contrast with your natural inclination to rely on your own abilities or moral achievements?*

SHARE GOD'S HEART

God has blessed you and heaped his lavish grace upon you through the death and resurrection of Jesus. You were saved, not because of your works but out of his sheer mercy and love. This reality should fill you with gratitude and awe, motivating you to share this good news with others.

- *Reread verse 6. How do you feel knowing that the Holy Spirit was "splashed over [you] richly"? What do you feel is a proper response to this act of God?*

- *God gives you the hope of eternal life (v. 7). This promise is unshakable. When you internalize the hope of eternal life, how does that change your relationships with those around you? What's truly at stake when you consider those around you who don't know or understand the fullness and power of God's grace and salvation through Jesus?*

- *Remember that sharing God's heart for others is an overflow from your relationship with him. God didn't save you and then leave you on your own to figure things out. Instead, he sent you the Holy Spirit so that you could be renewed (v. 6). How can you be prepared to not only share that overflow with others but also be ready to answer any questions they might have?*

Talking It Out

1. The hymn in Titus 3 is God-centered. It celebrates what God has done and will yet do for us. What are the songs like in your church gatherings? What do they teach?

2. Using Titus 3:4–7, what would you point to in this song to help you address some excuses people often give for rejecting the gospel? Here are a few of these excuses: "I need to clean up my life before God will accept me"; "I can save myself"; "I don't need to be saved because I'm good enough"; and "God is too busy to care about me."

3. Look back to Titus 3:3. How does the hymn in verses 4–7 relate to what Paul said in verse 3? Does it seem that people need to be reminded of how bad they are for them to better appreciate what God has done for them in Christ? Discuss your answers.

LESSON 9

Good Works and Good Friends

(Titus 3:8–15)

The last few verses of Titus 3 mark the closing portion of Paul's letter to Titus, where the apostle offered a final series of instructions and exhortations, reemphasizing good works, sound doctrine, and fruitful Christian lives. Now, Paul has already discussed his desire for Christian leaders to stand out from the crowd through noble living (2:7). He reemphasized this when he called on Christians to "devote themselves to doing good works" (3:8) as he brought his letter to a close.

Doing Good

- *Read Titus 3:8. When Paul mentioned "these truths," what has he just talked about that would constitute those truths (vv. 4–7)?*

- *What, then, is the relationship between salvation and good works?*

- *What did Paul see as the value of Christians doing what is good and right?*

- *What do you see as the value of Christians doing good works? Has this proven true in your life? Explain your answer.*

Avoiding Divisiveness

- *Paul turned from talking about good works to dealing with divisiveness. What did he identify as divisive among the Cretans (v. 9)?*

Did you notice that each of these divisive debates concerned the Law—that is, the Mosaic Law as expressed in the Pentateuch, the first five books of the Old Testament? Now, there's some great content in those Bible books, including the creation of the world, the fall of humanity, the Noahic flood, God's choice of Abraham and blessing upon him, the liberation of the Hebrews from Egyptian slavery, the revelation of the law for Jewish life, the wilderness wandering, and the preparation of the Hebrews to conquer the promised land. But over the centuries, including into Paul's day, the Jews had all kinds of disagreements over how to interpret and apply the Pentateuch. And they posed some of those divisive issues to Jesus in attempts to get him to take sides or to trap him in a dilemma. The aim was to compel him to take a position that would put him at odds with one of the rival Jewish factions or, even better, with the Roman authorities (Matthew 12:9–15; 22:15–46). But Jesus outsmarted these maneuvers at every turn, and as a result, his critics eventually stopped engaging him on matters concerning the Old Testament (Matthew 22:46).[51]

Now, when Jesus was no longer around, his Jewish critics dogged his followers, often going after them with false charges of blasphemy (Acts 13:44–51; 4:1–3; 5:17–40). Added to them were gentile critics who became upset because Christian teaching and practice threatened businesses that made money from pagan worship (see Acts 19:23–30). While some arguments and claims needed to be answered,[52] others were silly and pointless, not benefiting anyone—not in reality anyway. It was senseless inquiries, speculations, and arguments such as these that Paul wanted Christians to avoid.

- *What would you regard as senseless, pointless quarrels, debates, or criticisms that are unbeneficial and even divisive?*

- *Have you tried to engage any of these kinds of arguments and claims? If so, how did that go? Did it turn out well for anyone?*

- *What do you see as the danger of irrelevant or speculative discussions that distract from the core message of the gospel?*

THE BACKSTORY

One of the useless matters Paul mentioned is genealogies (Titus 3:9). In this case, a fixation on genealogies refers to a preoccupation with detailed genealogical discussions or arguments that have no practical or spiritual benefit for believers. In the first century, genealogies were important, especially in Jewish and Hellenistic contexts. In Judaism, certain genealogies were seen as essential for establishing a person's legitimacy (establishing whether one was a legitimate priest, of Davidic descent, etc.). However, here Paul didn't deny the historical value of genealogies. Instead, he didn't want them to become distractions from the core message of the gospel. Moreover, in the early church, some groups (particularly Jewish Christians) might have focused heavily on genealogies, trying to trace a lineage to prove spiritual superiority or legitimacy. In the case of Titus 3:9, then, Paul warned against such distractions because they diverted attention away from the essentials of faith and godly living. As Bible scholar William M. Ramsay noted:

> Paul's rejection of genealogies in Titus 3:9 points to a concern about speculative and unfruitful debates that were leading to divisiveness. These genealogies, likely of Jewish origin, could be used to assert spiritual superiority but do not contribute to the edification of the church or the advancement of the gospel.[53]

Handling Divisive People

In verses 10–11, Paul continued his warnings and gave some specific instructions for repeat offenders—those who have been warned multiple times and eschew correction. Paul wrote, "After a first and second warning, have nothing more to do with a divisive person who refuses to be corrected. For you know that such a one is entwined with his sin and stands self-condemned."

- *What was Paul's counsel for how to deal with a recalcitrant divisive person (v. 10)?*

- *Why did Paul believe that this was the best approach for handling such a person (v. 11)?*

- *What do you think could be the danger of letting those who sow division in the church go unchecked?*

Direction for Coworkers

In verses 12–15, Paul wrapped up his letter to Titus by giving him instructions on what he was to do for various coworkers of Paul.

- *Paul told Titus that he would be sending two men to him. Who were they (v. 12 and footnotes 'e' and 'f' for this verse)?*

- *After these men arrived in Crete, where was Titus supposed to go, and who would be there waiting for him (v. 12 and footnote 'g' for this verse)?*

- *Paul then mentioned two more men. Who were they, and what was Titus to do for them (v. 13 and footnotes 'h' and 'i' for this verse)?*

According to Bible commentator D. Edmond Hiebert, "Zenas and Apollos are almost certainly the bearers of this letter."[54] In other words, Titus received his letter from Paul by the hands of Zenas and Apollos, two of Paul's coworkers.

- *In verse 13, Paul encouraged Titus to provide "a generous send-off" and "what they need." What benefits of Christian fellowship are displayed here?*

- *Ministry is certainly a team effort. Why is it important for Christians to support each other in their service to Christ?*

Last Words

Paul brought his letter to a close by focusing on the believers under Titus' care.

- *What did Paul want Titus to encourage the Cretan Christians to do (v. 14)?*

- *How does this final exhortation tie into what Paul said elsewhere in his letter on this topic?*

- *Paul then shared greetings from those who were with him and asked Titus to greet those who were with him (v. 15). What did Paul then add that he desired for all who were in the Cretan churches?*

EXPERIENCE GOD'S HEART

Titus 3:8–15 offers some powerful insights about living out the gospel in practical ways, reflecting God's heart in how you should interact with others, and embracing God's grace and love.

- *According to verse 8, "those who believe in God will be careful to devote themselves to doing good works." How does this instruction connect with how you personally experience the heart of God? Do you feel there is a connection between devotion to good works and the way God has demonstrated his love and care toward you?*

SHARE GOD'S HEART

- *How does the emphasis on good works in Titus 3:8 reflect the heart of God toward others, especially those in need, and how can engaging in good works be a way of demonstrating God's love, mercy, and grace to the world around you?*

- *In verses 10–11, Paul advised rejecting a divisive person. How does this reflect God's heart for the church and for truth?*

- *Read verse 14. What are some examples of "meeting the urgent needs of others"? In your own experience, how have you shared God's heart by meeting the needs of others?*

Talking It Out

1. If you had to pick just one overarching theme for Paul's letter to Titus, what would it be? Why?

2. Even though Titus is only three chapters, Paul mentioned sound doctrine and good works multiple times. What do you see as the main connections between sound doctrine and good works?

3. Reread Titus 3:9–11. How have you handled disputes between other Christians in the past? Have you ever had a serious dispute with another Christian? How did you handle it? Do you think Paul would agree that you handled it well?

4. Paul clearly had some individuals around him on whom he depended and highly regarded. His ministry efforts were team-oriented. Discuss the benefits and drawbacks of team ministry as opposed to single-person ministry. Are both useful approaches, or do you think one is better than the other?

LESSON 10

Introduction to Philemon

(Philemon 1–3)

Philemon is a letter that was written with reconciliation in mind. You could even call it a love letter, though the idea behind the letter has nothing to do with romance. Rather, the letter is all about loving forgiveness—forgiveness founded in the love of Jesus.

Authorship, Date, and Recipient

The letter of Philemon came from the apostle Paul and his ministry partner Timothy (Philemon 1). The writer of the letter is Paul (v. 19). As Bible scholar Donald Guthrie put it, "in this brief epistle we are listening to the authentic tones of Paul's own pleading."[55]

Paul likely wrote this letter during his first imprisonment in Rome, around AD 60–61 (Acts 28:16–31). Because of this letter's close connection to the Colossians letter, Donald Guthrie said that this fact "makes it virtually certain that the two epistles belong to the same period." Moreover, Paul's mention of Tychicus and Onesimus (the slave at the center of Philemon) in his letter to the Colossians (Colossians 4:7–9) strongly supports the theory that "Tychicus accompanied by Onesimus took them both [the two epistles] to Colossae at the same time."[56] In fact, Onesimus was a native of Colossae (4:9), and he was also a slave owned by Philemon.

Paul's Philemon letter was written to Philemon but not only

to him. Paul also addressed his letter to the church that met in Philemon's house, as well as to Apphia and Archippus (Philemon 1–2). It's believed that Apphia was Philemon's wife.[57] Paul included her because her decision about Onesimus and his fate mattered as much as her husband's. As Bible commentator D. Edmond Hiebert noted, Apphia was "as much a party to the decision as her husband, because according to the custom of the time, she had day-to-day responsibility for the slaves" in their household.[58] As for Archippus, he was likely one of the leading figures in Philemon's church gathering (Colossians 4:17), and he could have been Philemon's son.[59] Paul referred to him as "our fellow soldier" in ministry (Philemon 2). Still, as the letter unfolds, it becomes clear that the first-named recipient, Philemon, is the primary focus, and the main subject is his runaway slave, Onesimus.

- *Turn now to the letter of Philemon and read through its twenty-three verses. Jot down at least three things that stand out to you in this brief letter.*

- *Now turn to Colossians 4:9. What do you learn there about Onesimus?*

- *Finally, return to Philemon and read verse 3. What blessing did Paul make for all of the recipients of his letter?*

Themes

Paul's letter of Philemon exhibits three major themes: Christian belonging in a common faith, the love of Christ performed, and slavery influenced by brotherhood. Let's look at each theme more closely.

Christian Belonging in a Common Faith

Paul's letter, while addressing an issue with Philemon, was meant to be read by the entire Christian community that met at Philemon's home. Why was a matter involving Philemon also something that concerned that church? As TPT's introductory material says,

> one of the enduring, relevant teachings of this letter is that our private business is a matter for the believing community since we belong to one another in a common faith.…When people commit themselves to Christ, they are also committing themselves to a community. They bind themselves and become identified with one another so that they receive both the benefits and responsibilities of that "belonging."[60]

We belong, not only to Christ, but also to the community of fellow followers of Christ. There's no Lone Ranger Christianity, no rugged individualism when it comes to being a Christian disciple. In Philemon, the matter at hand concerned two followers of Christ: Philemon and Onesimus. And both of them were part of the same Christian community. So their relational issues concerned the entire church body, not just the two of them.

- *In the context of Philemon, explain what Paul meant when he wrote this in Romans 12:5: "And so it is in the body of Christ. For though we are many, we've all been mingled into one body in Christ. This means that we are all vitally joined to one another, with each contributing to the others."*

- *In your local church, have you ever faced an issue between fellow believers that needed the attention of the whole church, that just couldn't be left between those believers to work out in privacy? If so, what was the issue at hand? How was it handled? How did it work out?*

- *If you have not had such a matter handled in your church, what kinds of issues between Christians do you think should warrant the involvement of your church's members? Why so?*

The Love of Christ Performed

The tone of Philemon is one in which every word is saturated with the love of Christ. Paul wanted Philemon to consider Onesimus just as Jesus considers us: forgiven, loved, precious, worthy, and inherently valuable. Christians are to regard one another just as Jesus regards them.

- *What does it mean to forgive someone?*

- *Are all sins forgivable? If not, which ones are exempt and why?*

- *Must forgiveness always lead to the restoration of the relationship? Is restoration always possible, much less achievable? Is it sometimes better not to seek restoration? If so, when might that be?*

- *Can the offended love the offender and still mistrust the offender? Consider in your answer what John said about Jesus in his gospel (2:23–25). How might this affect reconciliation thoughts and attempts?*

Slavery Influenced by Brotherhood

Slavery is the blaring issue in the relationship between Philemon and Onesimus. But Paul didn't broach the issue. Onesimus' status as a slave was simply an unavoidable social reality. And while Paul did press Philemon to "welcome him no longer as a slave, but more than that, as a dearly loved brother" (v. 16), for Paul, the important facet of their relationship was that of two followers of Jesus walking out their relationship in forgiveness.

THE BACKSTORY

The issue of slavery during the time of the apostle Paul was complex, deeply rooted in ancient social, economic, and cultural structures worldwide. Slavery was an accepted institution in the Roman Empire, which controlled the Mediterranean world and much of what we know as Europe.

Slavery was definitely an integral part of Roman society, and it was the cornerstone of the Roman economy. For example, slaves could be found as domestic workers, agricultural laborers, miners, skilled craftsmen, doctors, accountants, business managers, gladiators, and even tutors for wealthy Roman families. They had no personal legal rights and were considered property under Roman law. Some slaves were treated relatively well, particularly in wealthy households, while others, particularly those in mines or on large estates, suffered brutal conditions. Overall, "slavery was essential to the economy of the Roman Empire. It was the basic labor force for a variety of tasks: in the home, on the farm, in workshops, and in mines. Without slaves, the entire structure of Roman society would have collapsed."[61]

You read in Titus 2:9–10 how Christian slaves should act, and in 1 Timothy 6:1–2, in particular, Paul addressed how slaves should treat their masters. Still, Paul never explicitly condemned the institution of slavery. Bible scholar N. T. Wright noted the following with regard to Paul's view of slaves in the Christian community: "Paul's central claim was that in Christ, social distinctions were irrelevant. Slave and free, Jew and Gentile, male and female—none of these mattered for those who were in Christ."[62] Moreover, in at least Philemon according to Donald Guthrie,

> Paul transforms the character of the master-slave relationship. Onesimus is returning no longer as a slave but as a dear brother (verse 16). It is clearly incongruous for a Christian master to 'own' a brother in Christ in the contemporary sense of the

> word, and although the existing order of society could not be immediately changed by Christianity without a political revolution (which was contrary to Christian principles), the Christian master-slave relationship was so transformed from within that it was bound to lead ultimately to the abolition of the system.[63]

- *How was slavery different in the ancient world of Paul, Philemon, and Onesimus compared with what you know about slavery in the United States in the 1700s and 1800s?*

- *Reread the quote from N. T. Wright. Do you agree or disagree with Paul's stance when it comes to social distinctions? Why or why not?*

- *Have you ever defended someone or spoken up for someone on their behalf? What's the story behind your experience? What was the result, and what did you learn from the experience?*

EXPERIENCE GOD'S HEART

- *What is your attitude toward fellow Christians? Do you regard some more highly than others? Do you treat them differently? Why or why not?*

- *How do you handle disputes in the body of Christ? What is your standard for your own behavior in such matters?*

SHARE GOD'S HEART

- *Paul regarded Philemon as a "precious friend and companion" in ministry (Philemon 1). Do you have Christian friends? How would you describe them?*

- *Take some time right now to pray for your friends. You might also consider connecting with them and letting them know how you feel about them and how important they are to you. Friendship matters.*

Talking It Out

1. Slavery is still practiced today. Even in countries that have abolished its legal practice, it can still have a presence criminally. And, for the most part, its ongoing practice is tied to economics. Conduct some research on this and discuss your findings. You can discover some useful information on the internet.[64]

2. Over the centuries, Christians worked to free slaves, often purchasing them and then setting them free. And Christians in the United Kingdom and the United States did lead the effort to abolish slavery. Key to their efforts against slavery was the biblical teaching that human beings were created as God's image-bearers (Genesis 1:26–27), which gave them intrinsic worth. Christians also recognized God's love for the world and his Son's sacrifice for the sins of all peoples (John 3:16). For these reasons and others, Christians maintained that all human beings should be free and treated with respect. It took a long time for these beliefs to be worked out culturally and politically, but when and where they took hold, slavery suffered setbacks and eventually came to an end. Check out some reliable resources on slavery through the centuries, including those mentioned in the endnote at the end of this statement.[65] Discuss what you learned. You might also consider what you can do to address slavery today. Unfortunately, this practice continues in various parts of the world.

LESSON 11

Grateful for You

(Philemon 4–7)

For what and whom are you grateful? Unbelievers are marked by ingratitude, especially when it comes to what God has given them (Romans 1:21). As a Christian, does gratitude mark you? Are you thankful for God's provision in your life, for his grace and mercy and gifts? Do you appreciate the sacrifices that other people have made for you? The opportunities that have come your way? The comfort others have provided? The wisdom passed on to you? The lessons you have learned?

We all know that life's journey is difficult at times. And that includes serving God. The apostle Paul certainly knew this. Here's a list of hard times that he recorded in 2 Corinthians 11:23–27:

> I have worked much harder for God, taken more beatings, and been dragged to more prisons than they. I've been flogged excessively, multiple times, even to the point of death. Five times I've received thirty-nine lashes from the Jewish leaders. Three times I experienced being beaten with rods. Once they stoned me. Three times I've been shipwrecked; for an entire night and a day I was adrift in the open sea. In my difficult travels I've faced many

> dangerous situations: perilous rivers, robbers, foreigners, and even my own people. I've survived deadly peril in the city, in the wilderness, with storms at sea, and with spies posing as believers. I've toiled to the point of exhaustion and gone through many sleepless nights. I've frequently been deprived of food and water, left hungry and shivering out in the cold, lacking proper clothing.

Your journey and ministry service may be less harsh, but you still might bear some scars. Wounds can run deep. Nevertheless, whatever we have endured, we have received so much more, including the promise of everlasting life with God our Lord and Savior. Paul certainly knew this. In fact, he even encouraged believers to "make your life a prayer. And in the midst of everything be always giving thanks, for this is God's perfect plan for you in Christ Jesus" (1 Thessalonians 5:17). Paul lived his life as a Christian exuding gratitude.

- *Let's start this lesson by taking time to read Philemon 4–7. Note below what you learn here about Paul's thankfulness.*

Gratitude and Prayer

In verses 4–7, Paul mixed prayer and gratitude, both of which he directed at his dear friend Philemon. Paul was deeply thankful for Philemon, and he wanted Philemon to know that he was praying for him. As we study these verses, we want to take to heart Paul's abiding appreciation for Philemon and prayers for him and see what we can learn about gratitude and how to pray.

Paul's prayer and expressions of gratitude have three main parts: (1) thanking God, (2) asking God, and (3) expressing gratitude for outcomes.

1) Thanking God

- *Read verses 4 and 5. To whom was Paul thankful and for what?*

- *Given what you've learned about Philemon here, how is your faith in the Lord Jesus? How would you describe it? What report do you think others might give about your faith in Christ?*

- *How much do you love fellow Christians in your church and larger community? What do you think others would report about your love for other believers?*

- *Given the reason Paul wrote this letter to Philemon, why do you suppose he brought to the foreground what was reported about Philemon?*

- *What are you grateful for when it comes to your growth in the Christian life? Take time now to express your gratitude to God for how far he has brought you and for his promise to make you fully like Jesus Christ.*

2) Asking God

- *Paul then told Philemon what he would be offering up to God in prayer for him (v. 6). For what did Paul pray?*

- *What do you think Paul meant by "the faith we share" (v. 6)? Is he talking about the trust both men have in Jesus? Or is he referring to the doctrinal content of their faith commitment? Explain your answer.*

- *Why is it important that we "deepen [our] understanding of every good thing that belongs to [us] in Christ" (v. 6)? In fact, what are some of those good things?*

- *What are some good things that we have in Christ that you need to understand much better than you now do?*

- *Do you know how to increase your understanding of those things? If you need some help, seek out a pastor, friend, or family member who may be able to provide the help you need. You may also find some assistance on a trusted internet site. Ask the Lord to guide you in your pursuit of what you need to better understand.*

3) Expressing Gratitude for Outcomes

- *In verse 7, Paul focused on Philemon's love and what it had produced. What outcomes did Paul highlight?*

- *What phrase did Paul use that showed his love for Philemon?*

- *Philemon and his family hosted a house church. How does that fact alone represent his servant-minded heart?*

- *Remember, Paul wrote Philemon from prison. How would news of Philemon's love serve as an encouragement to Paul, especially given his current circumstances?*

- *What do you suppose Paul meant when he said that because of Philemon, "the hearts of the believers have been greatly refreshed" (v. 7)? When have you felt refreshment from fellow Christians?*

- *What impact has your love had on others, especially on fellow believers?*

EXPERIENCE GOD'S HEART

- *Paul prayed for Philemon. Who are you praying for?*

- *Paul heard of the results of Philemon's love and faith. What outcomes are you hearing about in regard to those for whom you pray?*

- *How does learning about changes occurring in the individuals and groups for which you pray encourage you in your Christian life?*

- *As you reflect on Paul's words to Philemon in verses 4–7, what personal qualities or actions do you feel God is calling you to develop in order to better serve and love others in your community?*

- *How can you better cultivate a spirit of gratitude in your life, similar to Paul's thankfulness for Philemon? Is there anyone in your life you could acknowledge and appreciate more openly?*

SHARE GOD'S HEART

- *How can you actively seek to encourage and refresh those around you, reflecting God's desire for his people to support one another in their faith journeys?*

- *In what specific ways can you embody Christ's love in your interactions with others, especially those who may not be so easy to love?*

- *Paul mentioned that Philemon's faith brought him joy and encouragement. How can you be a better source of encouragement to those around you?*

Talking It Out

1. Paul was a praying man. And he prayed not just for his own needs but also for the needs of others. In fact, he prayed for their ongoing growth in Christ, including their deepening understanding of all the good things they had in Christ. Who comes to your mind who could benefit from your prayers? Spend time in prayer for this person or persons. Even if you don't know what their current needs are, you can still pray that they continue to grow toward Christlikeness and deepen their knowledge of and appreciation for the Lord and what he has promised us.

2. Paul began verses 4–7 by expressing his gratitude to God for Philemon. This highlights the importance of recognizing and appreciating the contributions of others in our spiritual lives. Make a list of a few people you could call, send a text, write an email, or send a letter to, just to let them know you are grateful to God for them.

3. Philemon 4–7 illustrates how love is foundational to ministry and community life. How can you better encourage others to cultivate loving relationships that reflect Christ's love in your church community?

LESSON 12

Paul's Appeal

(Philemon 8–25)

Proverbs tells us, "Nothing is more appealing than speaking beautiful, life-giving words. For they release sweetness to our souls" (16:24). One implication of this passage is that while what we say matters, how and when we say it matters too. We can tell the truth and hurt someone rather than facilitate healing. How much better it is to speak truthfully but in a way that's easier to receive and appreciate. The truth might be hard to swallow sometimes, but we need to do what we can to make it easier to digest.

Paul's appeal to Philemon to take back his runaway slave Onesimus is masterfully presented. Paul took a difficult situation and applied a Christian perspective that had redemption and reconciliation at its heart. You see, in the Roman Empire at that time, the slave owner decided the punishment for a slave's offense. Runaways were not protected by Roman law.[66] Slaves were "commonly beaten, as well as punished by branding and other mutilation."[67] Fugitive slaves could even be "put to tasks in which their life expectancy was very short."[68] So Onesimus faced an ugly outcome. He needed an advocate who could make a good case for him. And he got that in the apostle Paul.

- *Read Philemon 8–25, then jot down what stands out to you in these verses.*

Friendship Matters

- *Reread verses 8–12 and then answer the following questions:*

  What did Paul say he could have done but chose not to?

  What did Paul do instead and on what basis?

  Why do you imagine that making an appeal based on friendship is better than making one based on authority and command?

  What was Paul's condition at the time?

For whom did Paul make his "loving appeal" to Philemon, and who had this person come to be for Paul?

The Requested Outcome

Paul appealed to Philemon as a friend, a "dear brother" (v. 7), and a "companion" in ministry (v. 1). And he referred to Philemon's runaway slave as his spiritual "child" (v. 9–10) and "very heart" (v. 12), who became valuable to him and Philemon (v. 11). But Paul had not yet asked Philemon what he wanted from him—not until halfway through his letter.

- *What had Onesimus become for Paul in his gospel work (v. 13)?*

- *Because of his new value, where did Paul want Onesimus to remain (v. 13)?*

- *Rather than demand that Philemon acquiesce to Paul's desire (vv. 8, 14), what approach did Paul take and why (v. 9–10, 14)?*

- *Paul's appeal, coupled with Onesimus' new identity in Christ and role as Paul's ministry partner, required that Philemon see Onesimus much differently than he had before. What was the new view that Paul wanted Philemon to embrace (vv. 15–17)?*

Sharing the Cost

Letting a slave go in the ancient world meant enduring some economic loss. Slaves were the involuntary working class in the Roman Empire. Much of what the empire accomplished—for example, construction projects, mining precious minerals and stones, crop harvesting, advancing education, and improving physical health—was due to the slave workforce.[69] Paul, however, did not promise to purchase Onesimus' freedom. Instead, he promised to compensate Philemon on a related matter.

- *What did Paul promise to compensate Philemon for (vv. 18–19 and the TPT footnotes on these verses)?*

- *What did Paul mean when he said that Philemon owed him his "very self" (v. 19)? Would that be more valuable to Philemon than anything Onesimus might have taken?*

So rather than purchase Onesimus' freedom, Paul offered to share the cost another way. So Philemon would lose a slave and any income that slave helped to provide. And if he chose to treat Onesimus as a beloved brother in Christ, he would defy the Roman tradition of punishing fugitive slaves. Paul's request

> put Philemon in a precarious position indeed. In pleading for forgiveness and restitution for Onesimus without a punishment that was obvious to all, he was confronting the social and economic order head on. While he does not ask for manumission, even his request for clemency for Onesimus and hint of his assignment to Paul defied Roman tradition. By this plea Paul is also giving new dignity to the slave class.[70]

Paul's request was a tough one, and it was risky. Onesimus had to return to his master, hoping he would not be severely punished. Paul had to hope that his appeal to friendship would not turn his friend against him. Both Paul and Onesimus had to hope that the believers meeting in Philemon's house would receive the appeal as intended and not turn against both men.

Hope with Confidence

Now, Paul wasn't finished with his appeal.

- *What did he add to it (vv. 20–22)?*

- *What do you think Paul meant when he said, "Do even more than what I'm asking" (v. 21)? What more could Philemon do?*

Paul talked with confidence that his risk (and Onesimus') would produce positive results. According to the historical record outside of the New Testament, Paul's appeal paid off well. "Orthodox Church tradition tells us that Onesimus served Christ faithfully throughout his life and became the bishop of the church of Ephesus after Timothy's death."[71] Onesimus served his new master, Jesus Christ, well, and he must have done so as a freedman under Roman law.

Final Greetings and Blessing

Paul closed out his letter to Philemon with greetings from some of his partners in ministry (vv. 23–24):

> **Epaphras**—He must have shared imprisonment with Paul at the time since he's referred to as "my fellow prisoner" (v. 23). Epaphras was a leader in the Colossian church who later suffered martyrdom there (Colossians 1:7; 4:12–13).[72]
>
> **Mark**—This is the same believer who wrote the gospel of Mark. He was with Paul during his first imprisonment in Rome, and later he was with Peter in Babylon (1 Peter 5:13) and then with Timothy at Ephesus, at which time Paul requested Mark's presence in Rome during Paul's second imprisonment there (2 Timothy 4:11).[73]
>
> **Aristarchus**—He was a native of Thessalonica who became one of Paul's faithful companions on his third missionary journey. He went with Paul to Ephesus, "where he was seized and nearly killed in the tumult raised by the silversmiths under Demetrius (Acts 19:29)." From there he traveled with Paul to "Greece, then to Asia (20:4), and subsequently to Rome (27:2), to which he was sent as a prisoner, or he became one while there (Philem. 24), for Paul calls him his 'fellow prisoner' (Col. 4:10)."[74]
>
> **Demas**—He was also a companion of Paul during the apostle's first imprisonment at Rome

(Colossians 4:14). Later, however, Demas deserted Paul and "left to go to Thessalonica, for he [loved] his own life" (2 Timothy 4:10).

Luke—He is the author of the gospel that bears his name. A gentile, Luke was a physician who traveled with Paul and recounted some of those experiences in another book he wrote, Acts (note the "we" sections; e.g., Acts 16:10–17:1; 20:6–28:16). He was with Paul during his first imprisonment in Rome (Colossians 4:14), and he later remained with Paul even when some other companions left the apostle (2 Timothy 4:9–11).[75]

- *Do you have coworkers who you know would stick by you? If so, pray for them now, thanking God for them and asking him to strengthen them, inspire them, and gift them for the work you all share. If you lack the coworkers you need, ask the Lord to open the way for workers to come alongside you and give you what you need to accomplish what he has for you to do.*

EXPERIENCE GOD'S HEART

- *How God sees you is the way you should see yourself and others. How does Paul's request for Philemon to accept Onesimus as a brother in Christ rather than as a slave illustrate the way God sees you?*

- *Are you a risk taker? Paul sure was. He laid it all on the line, and while it probably wasn't that big of a deal for him to have Onesimus' back, it was a huge deal for Onesimus. When's the last time someone truly had your back? How'd it make you feel?*

- *Have you ever stepped out, taken a risk, to help someone who had messed up but showed clear signs of turning their life around? If so, what happened? How did it turn out? What did you learn from the experience?*

SHARE GOD'S HEART

- *In what ways can you emulate the example of Paul, Philemon, and Onesimus in your relationships with others? Do you need to pursue forgiveness, reconciliation, or apply some unconditional love to a situation in your life? Take some time to process, pray, and plan!*

Talking It Out

1. Paul appealed to Philemon out of love and friendship rather than command. Where can you apply such a principle in your own life right now?

2. Onesimus went from a runaway slave to a beloved brother in Christ. Even if his status as a slave couldn't change, he was beloved by Paul and eternally loved by God. What transformations have you seen in your life? And what transformations do you still hope to see?

3. Paul served as a strong advocate for Onesimus, going so far as to offer to pay off his debts. Have you ever advocated for anyone in your life in a similar way, or has anyone served as an advocate in a similar manner for you? Describe the situation and how it made you feel.

4. In Christ, there is no distinction between slave and free. Paul wrote this in Galatians 3:28: “And we no longer see each other in our former state—Jew or non-Jew, rich or poor, male or female—because we’re all one through our union with Jesus Christ.” How does Paul’s letter to Philemon illustrate this biblical principle?

5. Paul seems very confident in his letter, and he seems confident that Philemon’s actions will continue to bring him joy and refreshment. Why do you think Paul was so confident that Philemon would do the right thing?

Endnotes

1. Brian Simmons et al., "A Note to Readers," *The Passion Translation: The New Testament with Psalms, Proverbs, and Song of Songs* (Savage, MN: BroadStreet Publishing Group, 2020), ix.

2 John Whittaker, "Summary of Titus: Understanding the Basics of Titus in the Bible," Renew.org, accessed July 1, 2025, https://renew.org/summary-of-titus.

3 John MacArthur, "Titus," Blue Letter Bible, accessed June 3, 2025, https://www.blueletterbible.org/Comm/macarthur_john/bible-introductions.

4 The Bible reference in the original quotation is 2 Corinthians 13:18, which does not exist. We corrected it to 2 Corinthians 12:18, which is clearly the passage the author intended to reference.

5 Brian Dennert, "Who Was Titus?," Faith Church, August 22, 2023, https://wearefaith.org/blog/who-was-titus.

6 Hint: It's a laborious twelve-step process, and you're going to need to know how to use a welding torch (see Howard Fleischmann, "How to Fix a Bent Rim," WikiHow, last updated April 6, 2025, https://www.wikihow.com/Fix-a-Bent-Rim).

7 James Strong, "4245," *The New Strong's Expanded Dictionary of Bible Words* (Thomas Nelson, 2001), 1330.

8 G. R. Osborne, "Elder," in *Dictionary of Jesus and the Gospels*, eds. Joel B. Green and Scot McKnight (InterVarsity Press, 1992), 201.

9 Vincent P. Branick, *The House Church in the Writings of Paul* (Wipf and Stock, 1989), 15; A. Kenneth Curtis et al, *The 100 Most Important Events in Christian History* (Fleming H. Revell, 1991), 33.

10 D. J. Tidball, "Social Setting of Mission Churches," in *Dictionary of Paul and His Letters*, eds. Gerald F. Hawthorne and Ralph P. Martin (InterVarsity Press, 1993), 887.

11 See C. G. Kruse, "Ministry," in *Dictionary of Paul and His Letters*, 603–604; and Kevin Giles, *Patterns of Ministry Among the First Christians*, 2nd ed. (Cascade Books, 2017), chaps. 4 and 6.

12 Kruse, "Ministry," in *Dictionary of Paul and His Letters*, 603–604.

13 See David Gibson, "Why My Shepherd Carries a Rod," TGC, April 21, 2024, https://www.thegospelcoalition.org/article.

14 See John W. Ritenbaugh, "What the Bible Says about Function of Shepherd's Staff," Bibletools, accessed July 3, 2025, https://www.bibletools.org/index.cfm.

15 D. Edmond Hiebert, *Titus and Philemon* (Moody Press, 1957), 41.

16 Mike Ford, "What the Bible Says about Reputation of Cretans," Bibletools, accessed February 21, 2025, https://www.bibletools.org/index.cfm.

17 Hiebert, *Titus and Philemon*, 41.

18 Mark Cartwright, "Ancient Crete," *World History Encyclopedia*, February 2, 2017, https://www.worldhistory.org/crete.

19 Cartwright, "Ancient Crete," *World History Encyclopedia*.

20 For additional quotes by Groeschel, check out Goodreads.com.

21 James Strong, "1319," *The New Strong's Expanded Dictionary of Bible Words* (Thomas Nelson, 2001), 1042; Strong, "5198," 1422.

22 P. H. Towner, "Households and Household Codes," in *Dictionary of Paul and His Letters*, 417.

23 Towner, "Households and Household Codes," 417.

24 Towner, "Households and Household Codes," 417.

25 B. Van Elderen, "Titus," *The Zondervan Pictorial Encyclopedia of the Bible*, gen. ed. Merrill C. Tenney (Zondervan, 1976), vol. 5, 759.

26 Elderen, "Titus," 759. For more on the minister Titus, see F. F. Bruce's fine treatment in his book *The Pauline Circle* (William B. Eerdmans, 1985), chap. 8.

27 The phrase "enslaved or free" is the alternate translation found in TPT, the footnote for Galatians 3:28.

28 See the TPT footnote for Titus 2:9.

29 Lesley Adkins and Roy A. Adkins, *Handbook to Life in Ancient Rome* (Oxford University Press, 1994), 341; Michael Grant, *A Social History of Greece and Rome* (Charles Scribner's Sons, 1992), 102.

30 William L. Westermann, *The Slave Systems of Greek and Roman Antiquity* (The American Philosophical Society, 1955), chap. XIII.

31 Westermann, *The Slave Systems of Greek and Roman Antiquity*, 84; Adkins and Adkins, *Handbook to Life in Ancient Rome*, 341.

32 S. S. Bartchy, "Slave, Slavery," in *Dictionary of the Later New Testament and Its Developments*, eds. Ralph P. Martin and Peter H. Davids (InterVarsity Press, 1997), 1099.

33 Bartchy, "Slave, Slavery," 1098.

34 Adkins and Adkins, *Handbook to Life in Ancient Rome*, 342.

35 Adkins and Adkins, *Handbook to Life in Ancient Rome*, 342; A. A. Rupprecht, "Slave, Slavery," *Dictionary of Paul and His Letters*, 881.

36 Bartchy, "Slave, Slavery," 1099. See also Adkins and Adkins, *Handbook to Life in Ancient Rome*, 342.

37 Bartchy, "Slave, Slavery," 1099.

38 Adkins and Adkins, *Handbook to Life in Ancient Rome*, 342.

39 R. Tuente, "Slave, Servant, Captive, Prisoner, Freedman," *The New International Dictionary of New Testament Theology*, gen. ed. Colin Brown (Zondervan, 1978), vol. 3, 597.

40 See "Grace," *Nelson's New Illustrated Bible Dictionary* (Thomas Nelson, 1995).

41 This fuller understanding of the two natures of Jesus and their relationship to each other is clearly articulated in the Creed of Chalcedon (451). Here's one place you can find it online: "Chalcedonian Creed (A.D. 451)," CARM, accessed July 17, 2025, https://carm.org/creeds-and-confessions.

42 To learn more about how the church came to understand the divine-human aspects of Jesus, see Richard A. Norris, ed. and trans., *The Christological Controversy*, Sources of Early Christian Thought series (Fortress Press, 1980); St. Athanasius, *On the Incarnation*, rev. ed. (St. Vladimir's Orthodox Theological Seminary, 1953); John D. Hannah, *Our Legacy: The History of Christian Doctrine* (NavPress, 2001).

43 It seems like quite the idyllic place: http://www.hot-springs-village-arkansas.com.

44 Andrew Wallace-Hadrill, as quoted by Carolyn Osiek and David Balch, *Families in the New Testament World: Households and House Churches* (Westminster John Knox Press, 1997), 24.

45 Osiek and Balch, *Families in the New Testament World*, 25.

46 Osiek and Balch, *Families in the New Testament World*, 32.

47 Osiek and Balch, *Families in the New Testament World*, 30; Pierre A. Thomé, "Mithraism," *World History Encyclopaedia*, June 10, 2015, https://www.worldhistory.org/Mithraic_Mysteries.

48 To explore the issues that these questions raise about the relationship between the Christian and the state, see Miranda Zapor Cruz, *Faithful Politics: Ten Approaches to Christian Citizenship and Why It Matters* (InterVarsity Press, 2024); Norman L. Geisler, "Civil Disobedience," in *Christian Ethics: Contemporary Issues and Options*, 2nd ed. (Baker Academic, 2010); Hugo Rahner, *Church and State in Early Christianity* (Ignatius Press, 1992); Oscar Cullman, *The State in the New Testament*, rev. ed. (SCM Press, 1963).

49 For an excellent introduction to this phenomenon in Scripture, see R. P. Martin, "Hymns, Hymn Fragments, Songs, Spiritual Songs," in *Dictionary of Paul and His Letters*, 419–23. To learn more about early Christian hymnody and worship as a whole, see R. P. Martin, *Worship in the Early Church* (William B. Eerdmans, 1974).

50 Titus 3:4, TPT footnote 'f' for this passage.

51 To learn more about how Jesus used reason, story, and other methods to demonstrate the truths he taught and lived, see Norman L. Geisler and Patrick Zukeran, *The Apologetics of Jesus* (Baker Books, 2009); and Travis Dickinson, *Logic and the Way of Jesus* (B&H, 2022).

52 For example, Galatians is an answer to Judaizers who tried to bring Christians back under obedience to the regulations of the Mosaic law; Hebrews answers a number of arguments used to try to show that Jesus was not the supreme being or authority; and the Gospel of Matthew demonstrates that Jesus was the Messiah prophesied to come in the Old Testament. Also see F. F. Bruce, *The Defense of the Gospel in the New Testament*, rev. ed. (William B. Eerdmans, 1977).

53 William M. Ramsay, *The Pastoral Epistles*, The New International Commentary on the New Testament series (William B. Eerdmans, 1992), 157.

54 D. Edmond Hiebert, "Titus," in *The Expositor's Bible Commentary*, ed. Frank E. Gaebelein (Zondervan, 1978), vol. 11, 448.

55 Donald Guthrie, *New Testament Introduction*, 4th ed. (InterVarsity Press, 1990), 664.

56 Guthrie, *New Testament Introduction*, 664.

57 Philemon 2, TPT footnote 'c.'

58 D. Edmond Hiebert, "Philemon," 458.

59 Philemon 2, TPT footnote 'c.'

60 TPT, "Philemon: Introduction: Major Themes."

61 *Ancient Slavery and Modern Ideology* (Penguin Books, 1983), 24.

62 N. T. Wright, *Paul: A Biography* (SPKC Publishing, 2018), 125.

63 Guthrie, *New Testament Introduction*, 665–66. For more on slavery in the ancient Roman world, see Lesson 5, "The Backstory."

64 One such place is WorldAtlas, "Slavery Today: Countries with the Highest Prevalence of Modern Slaves," by James Karuga, June 10, 2019, https://www.worldatlas.com/articles.

65 To learn more about the history of slavery and Christianity's impact on it, check out any of these resources: "Tracing Christianity's Impact on Slavery through the Centuries," by Sharon James, October 7, 2023, at https://www.crossway.org/articles; Jeffrey B. Russell, "Christianity and Black Slavery," *Christian Research Institute*, updated February 19, 2025, https://www.equip.org/articles; D. James Kennedy and Jerry Newcomb, *What If Jesus Had Never Been Born?* (Thomas Nelson, 1994), 18–22.

66 Hiebert, "Philemon," 460.

67 Adkins and Adkins, *Handbook to Life in Ancient Rome*, 353.

68 Hiebert, "Philemon," 460.

69 Bartchy, "Slave, Slavery," 1098–99; Adkins and Adkins, *Handbook to Life in Ancient Rome*, 342.

70 Hiebert, "Philemon," 460.

71 TPT, "Philemon: Introduction: About Philemon."

72 Merrill F. Unger, "Epaphras," *The New Unger's Bible Dictionary* (Moody Press, 1988), 364.

73 Unger, "Mark," *The New Unger's Bible Dictionary*, 815.

74 Unger, "Aristarchus," *The New Unger's Bible Dictionary*, 102.

75 Unger, "Luke," *The New Unger's Bible Dictionary*, 787–88.